First STEPS
in Letterland®
by Lyn Wendon

Published by Letterland Ltd
Barton, Cambridge CB3 7AY
England

First Printing 1986
Second Printing (with revisions) 1988
Third Printing (with revisions) 1989
Fourth Printing (with revisions) 1991
Fifth Printing (with revisions) 1992
Sixth Printing (with revisions) 1994

ISBN 0 907345 14X

Letterland was devised by Lyn Wendon and is part
of the Pictogram System copyright © Lyn Wendon 1973–1994

Produced by Templar Publishing Ltd, Old King's Head Court
High Street, Dorking, Surrey.

Edited by A.J. Wood.
Designed by Alistair Carlisle.
Photography by Amy Lewandowski, Michael Little and John Melton
Artwork by Hayward Art Group, Jane Launchbury and Lyn Wendon

Colour separations by Positive Colour Ltd, Maldon, Essex.

Printed and bound in Great Britain by
Raithby, Lawrence & Co. Ltd., Leicester & London

Contents

Section 1

Section 2

Section 3

For important general principles of word structure such as the Magic E, Vowels Out Walking (**ai, ea, oa**, etc.), Witch Controlled Vowels (**aw, ow, ew**, etc.), Robber Controlled Vowels (**ar, er, ir, or, ur** and **oor, our** etc.) and others, see Programme 2.

Each new Pictogram and story will bring thousands of words into the children's reading vocabulary and simultaneously inform and guide their progress in spelling.

Barton Primary School, Cambridge

FOREWORD

I must have encountered Lyn Wendon's Letterland first at the time of the Bullock Report – *A Language for Life* – in which the urgency for an improvement in the teaching for literacy was first recognised as a matter for public concern.

I remember well the enthusiastic response to the Letterland characters of both children and teachers in the school where I was headmaster and particularly the interest of those members of staff who felt themselves ill-prepared to meet the new call for improvements in the teaching of reading. They welcomed the Hairy Hat Man, the Wicked Water Witch and all the other Pictogram characters, realising that by using the System they themselves acquired the background knowledge for improvements in teaching which perhaps they lacked. We found that the children soon learned to use the characters as aide-memoires for correct letter formation and quickly understood their function in words.

In the years since then I have watched the Pictogram System mature continuously, widening its scope until it fostered oracy skills and sentence structure as well as phonics and spelling. The presentation of Letterland, in this new edition, is a highly professional package, making the System manifestly easy to use. It will be welcomed widely, I am sure.

As a Primary Adviser since 1972 I have arranged many courses to introduce Pictograms and I have found that teachers have been stimulated and supported by the system. In particular, I have noted its tendency to introduce into classrooms a fresh spirit of adventure in learning letters and a happy collaboration between teachers and children in the language built around this learning. The underlying sense of imagination and fun actually fosters creative initiative in both teachers and children. The resulting artwork, original stories and dramatic presentations in many schools have borne testimony to the effectiveness of the approach.

Letterland straddles the ebb and flow of controversy concerning the best method for teaching literacy skills, and reading in particular. There are

4

strongly held and often irreconcilable views as to what is best, but I doubt if many teachers would quarrel with the recent U.S.A. Report of the Federal Commission on Reading – *Becoming a Nation of Readers* – which defines reading as "the process of constructing meaning from written texts".

Similarly, most teachers would agree that children should be helped to develop strategies for reading which include the use of many divers clues in order to *predict* meaning.

As they read predictively, children are helped by a knowledge of sound/symbol correspondences to check their predictions. They also need this knowledge to understand word construction, to support spelling and the development of dictionary skills.

Letterland is far more than just a phonic teaching system. The result of thorough research, it is designed to provide teachers with the broadest possible platform for attacking literacy in which phonic facts, reading for meaning, and sight word strategies, etc. are all accommodated.

It is my experience that the use of Letterland materials alongside a well-constructed reading programme provides an excellent basis for the development of competence in literacy. This is true whether the reading programme consists of a well-chosen reading scheme, together with non-scheme books, or a reading programme which emphasises only the use of non-scheme books.

Lyn Wendon is to be congratulated on this contribution to the available resources for teaching literacy.

**Peter Smith, Education Authority Primary Adviser,
Lecturer and author.**

Peter Smith.

How I came to Letterland

I was teaching Bettina, aged 7. She was a child of good ability but utterly hopeless at reading – let alone writing. Two years of classroom failure had severely demoralised her and she was becoming allergic to teachers. I was attempting a one-to-one rescue.

I switched sides. What could *we* do with those treacherous alphabet letters? They never behaved the way we expected! As soon as we learned their sound there they were making another.

We were comparing the letter **a**, as in 'apple', with the **a**, as in 'saw', and wondering *why* it changed its sound? "I know", cried Bettina. "There is a bad witch and she makes the apple taste horrible!"

It was an intriguing idea: a metaphor to explain a shift in sound. When I realised that we might substitute the word '**aw**ful' for Bettina's 'horrible' I became thoroughly alert. Bettina, of course, had no way of knowing that an **a** followed by a **w** invariably altered the sound of **a**. But that was the point. Now she never would need to learn such an unappetising and abstract rule, provided she could use the word '**aw**ful' as a mnemonic for the sound shift. An awful witch was just the ticket. I drew a stick figure for a witch standing on the **w** making the apple taste **aw**ful and we named her the Wicked Witch.

Bettina had given me a way to hold her attention. Could this be widened into a general teaching strategy which just might take the pain out of her learning? I tried many more figures across the alphabet (which I later called Pictograms) and gave them all alliterative names.

To my own great astonishment, the better part – or rather, the worst part – of letter behaviour could be explained in this novel style. I was able to dispense with burdensome phonic rules and rote learning.

The complexities of the written language could be explained in fun and fantasy in a place which I called Letterland. Taught early enough, special learning difficulties, such as Bettina's, might never become a serious or protracted problem.

But Letterland really came into its own as teachers of infants discovered that by adopting this approach as *their* way of speaking about letter behaviour they did indeed bring about a swifter passage to literacy, both for the normal children *and* for those with special needs in their classrooms.

While Bettina has been growing into a self-assured young woman 'her' Wicked Witch, joined by Naughty Nick, the Robber Brothers, the Easy Magic Man, the Hairy Hat Man, Golden Girl, Poor Peter and all the others who populate the world of Letterland, has spread into infant schools throughout the country.

That is how this book came to be written, thanks to Bettina and innumerable teaching friends and colleagues whose own experience of Letterland has since helped to enrich this book.

Lyn Wendon

ACKNOWLEDGEMENTS

I have never known such a place as Letterland for making friends! I cannot count the number of productive hours on the telephone, the letters and the happy encounters with teachers and advisers whose enthusiasm and constructive suggestions have spurred me on.

I owe special acknowledgements to:

Carol Lycett, Head Teacher, Lees Hill Infants, Barnsley, Yorks, who has planned and co-authored the 'Listen and Write' sheets with me.

Roger Pope, formerly Music Adviser for North Hertfordshire, now Assistant Director of Studies at Trinity College of Music, London, who has composed many fine melodies for Letterland Audio Tape No. 1 and accompanying Songbook.

Barbara Pointon, Head of Music Department, Homerton College, Cambridge, whose songs (carried forward on to the tape from the original Pictogram System Set I) are already known and enjoyed by so many children.

Vivien Stone, Language Post teacher, Seagrave Primary School, Strelley, Notts., who has planned and co-authored the handwriting verses on the tape, for chanting, singing and reading.

Mary Boulton, remedial teacher at Gamlingay Primary School, Cambs., lecturer and Honorary Editor of Letterland News, for her continuous support, and liaison with many Letterland teachers.

Above all, I have much valued the creative input of Graham Holbrow, Head Teacher of Hatherleigh Primary, Devon, who first saw the potentials in my Pictograms for play acting – thereby opening up a whole new range of possibilities for the System.

The teaching profession is one of the last refuges of altruism. Each person mentioned in the following list has been of special help to me, either because of their creative implementation of the system, or for their pivotal comments, constructive criticism and care in reporting back on field trials, or for their willingness to share their ever growing expertise by accepting invitations to run courses on Letterland, or to report their experience in Letterland News, or to permit themselves to be recorded on video.

I have not included the names of Advisers but my debt extends to many of them as well.

I hope I may be forgiven for inadvertent omissions in recording my debt to so many creative spirits who have taken up citizenship in Letterland and helped me to compile all that is now known about it. We have all been explorers together.

My long list is headed by the teachers who appear on the Letterland Videos 'The Way to Letterland', Tapes 1, 2 and 3:

Graham Holbrow, H.T., Hatherleigh Primary, Nr. Okehampton, Devon.
Peggy Sorum, nee Hicks, H.T., Selborne 1st & Middle School, Middx.
Miriam Jones, Pinkwell Junior, Hayes, Middx.
Keith Nicholson, Alfred Street Primary, Rushden, Northants.
Marguerite Roberts, Whittlesford Primary, Cambs.
Clare Stratton, nee Grigson, English Speaking School, Dubai, U.A.E.
Anne Whitlam, H.T., Yeading Infants, Hayes, Middx.

Margaret Alcorn, Child Guidance Centre, Ayr, Scotland.
Brenda Barnard, Deputy Head, Caldmore Primary, Walsall, W. Midlands.
Jennifer Barrett, Senior Speech Therapist, Castlegate Clinic, Lewes, E. Sussex.
Cynthia Beckett and Judy Manson, Callowbrook First, Rubery, Birmingham.
Sheila Bonner, Deputy Head (ret'd.), George Palmer Infants, Reading, Berks.
Joan Boots and Janeen Daniels, Walmley 1st School, W. Midlands.
Violet Brand, Author/Lecturer, Specialist Teacher, Watford, Herts.
Marlene Broadhead, Shepherds Infants, Rickmansworth, Herts.
Enid Brydon, H.T., Trent Vale Infants, Beeston Rylands, Notts.
Marie Chalmers and Vel Williams, Hallfield Infants, London.
Barbara Chasewood, H.T., Sheila Brown and Polly Williams, Hermitage 1st, Surrey.
Dr. Kathy Clem, Cambridge, Massachusetts, U.S.A.
Gillian Cook, Bassetlaw (Special) School, Worksop, Notts.
Mary Davis, Hamworthy 1st School, Nr. Poole, Dorset.
Hilary Dumbrill, Speech Therapist, Community Services, Brighton.
Sue Dyble, H.T., Fair View Infants, Gillingham, Kent.
Ann England, Springmead J.M.I., Welwyn Garden City, Herts.
Cynthia Evans, H.T., Sytchampton Endowed School, Stourport, Worcs.
June Everall, Jean Stone, Ashcroft Infants, Tamworth, Staffs.
Jenny Evers, Prae Wood J.M.I., St. Albans, Herts.
J. Fitzgerald, H.T., Cherry Lane Infants, West Drayton, Middx.
Rita Gerrard, H.T., Petersfield County Infants, Hants.
Cheryl Gosling, H.T., Joan Gooch, Paulsgrove East 1st, Portsmouth, Hants.
Margaret Goode, H.T. (ret'd.), Doxey 1st, Stafford.
Eileen Golby, Claterbridge Bebington Hospital School, Wirral, Merseyside.
Barbara Green, Dorchester Primary, Worcester Park, Surrey.
Geraldine Gysin-Connelly, International School, Basel, Switzerland.
Ann Hanson, Heatherside Infants, Fleet, Hampshire.
Mary Howard, H.T., Audrey Hagg, Terrington St. Clement Infants, Norfolk.
Cath Humphries, Head of Lower School, Aynsley (Special) School, Stoke on Trent.
Patricia Jiggens, HT, Downsview C.P. Infants, Swanley, Kent.
Ian Lane, H.T., Welford Primary, Handsworth, Birmingham.
Linda Lees, Anthea Prosser, St. John's C. of E., Kidderminster, W. Midlands.
Deidre Leeming, Marlfield Farm 1st, Redditch, Worcs.
Julia Lumley, Daphne Thomas, Waterbeach Community Primary, Cambs.
Judith Mallon, Moor Lane Junior, Chessington, Surrey.
Vivian Mansfield, Nursery School Head, Seattle, Washington, U.S.A.
Jane Marsden, Al Khubairat Community School, Abu Dhabi, U.A.E.
Maria Matthews, Newington Infants, Ramsgate, Kent.
Winifred Meeham, H.T., St. Annes J.M.I. R.C., Weeping Cross, Staffs.

Joyce Milne, Archibald First School, Newcastle upon Tyne.
Pat Minton, Marillac House Special School, Brighton, Victoria, Australia.
Eileen Nesworthy, Midmore Primary School, Hull, N. Humberside.
Diane Nettleton, Fylingdales C. of E., Whitby, N. Yorks.
Joyce New, H.T., Broadwater Infants, Tooting, London.
Vivien Norman, Western Road, County Primary, Lewes, Sussex.
Stephanie Orford, Senior Speech Therapist, Fleming (Special) School, Belfast.
Doreen Pepper, H.T., Merland Rise First, Epsom, Surrey.
Rita Pike, H.T., Miers Court Primary, Gillingham, Kent.
Margaret Pope, H.T., Strathmore Infants, Hitchin, Herts.
Carolyn Poulter, H.T., High Down Infants School, Portishead, Bristol.
Diana Powder-Kent, H.T., St. Mary's Infants, Cumbria.
Rhoda Poyser, H.T., Blakenall Heath Primary, Leamore, Walsall.
Vera Quin, St. Thomas Hospital Learning Difficulties Clinic, London S.E.1.
Jean A. Raffe, H.T., Hackbridge Infants, Wallington, Surrey.
Pauline Rowse, Deputy Head, Bradley Barton Primary, Newton Abbot, Devon.
Shirley Rump, H.T., Eastwick County First, Leatherhead, Surrey.
Jill Salis, St. Etheldredas County Infants, Ely, Cambs.
Jenny Samways, Lytchett Matravers Primary, Devon.
Sandra Sanders, Shields Elementary School, San Jose, California, U.S.A.
Ann Stoker, H.T., Hamsey Green C. 1st, Warlingham, Surrey.
Christine Stophair, St. Lawrence 1st, Gnosall, Stafford.
Judith Sharman, Head of Infants, Tarvin Primary, Cheshire.
D.P. Stone, H.T., St. Peter's C.E. Primary, Tunbridge Wells, Kent.
Jill Stringer, Deputy Head, Fawbert and Barnard Primary, Old Harlow, Essex.
Wyn Unsworth, Head of Infants, Bar Hill Primary, Cambs.
Vi Urwin, Head of Infants, Brampton Junior School, Huntingdon, Cambs.
Iris Vogeli, H.T., Magdalen Gates 1st, Norwich.
Hazel Waddup, H.T., Hangleton 1st School, Hove, E. Sussex.
Leslie Walden, H.T., Kate Ellis, Bishop Wilson C.E. Primary, Birmingham.
Doreen Wakeford, Farnborough Grange Junior and Infants, Farnborough, Hants.
Joanna Watkins, Head of Infants, R.A.F. Wildenrath, W. Germany.
Deborah Webster, Deputy Head, Hillmorton Paddox Ct. Combined, Rugby, Warks.
S.A. Wells, H.T., Goldsworth 1st, Woking, Surrey.
Eileen Wheeler, Somerset College, Mudgeeraba, Queensland, Australia.
Norry Williams, H.T., (up to 1986), Cannock Nursery, Staffs.
Sheila Williams, H.,T., Whitehouse Common First, Birmingham.

Last but not least, special gratitude for unstinting help (and fearless criticism) goes to Richard Carlisle of Templar Publishing and to Mandy Wood, its editorial director, for seeing me through the hazards of print. I have caused them many a sigh.

Section 1

If the teaching of reading were easy there would be no need for such a book as this. Nor would Letterland have been invented if the practice of beginning with old style phonic instruction had not been justly abandoned.

What follows is an attempt to help even very young children to become aware of the life blood coursing through words, letter by letter, beat by beat by beat, without risk that the ultimate goal, delight in our written language, dies along the way!

This section introduces the concepts, the materials and the practices which are available to the Letterland teacher.

Letterland: An Overview

FIRST STEPS IN LETTERLAND introduces a special place called Letterland and the alphabet characters who live there. You and the children explore Letterland together to discover and observe letter behaviour in words.

At one level, Letterland is simply fun. This is how children will first perceive it. But beneath the surface, almost subliminally, there is a systematic and structured course of learning, containing the following major elements.

- Emphasis on language:
  listening, speaking, communicating
- Phonic skills
- Whole-word recognition skills
- Sentence awareness
- Reading for meaning
- Development of reading and spelling together
- Early creative writing

Emphasis on Language

The teaching vehicle in Letterland is the telling of stories. You encourage the children to listen carefully to the stories so that they can ask questions and speculate with you about letters, their shapes, their sounds, and relationships between them.

Language initiative passes to the children as you fuel their curiosity about Letterland, leading them to participate in the story-telling and to explore Letterland in their imaginations. They recount the stories and, as they do so, they reinforce their learning.

You extend the children's participation by a variety of supplemental activities: play-acting, reciting rhymes, playing alliterative games, singing, Letterland art and crafts, and by using handwriting verses and worksheets.

Phonic Skills

Children discover the letters' sounds simply by *starting* to pronounce each Pictogram character's name. You strengthen this discovery by showing the children how to picture code each letter shape. This picture coding helps them to 'see' the letters' sounds. You can code some or all letters.

his sea shells

The effect is simultaneous reinforcement of both shape and sound in any given word.

Welcome to Letterland

Ashcroft Infants School, Tamworth, Staffs.

Whole Word Recognition

The STEPS encourage some whole-word recognition from the start. The alliterative character names (Clever Cat, Eddy Elephant, Golden Girl, Poor Peter and so on) include no less than 40 common words which young readers will soon recognise as sight words in other contexts as well.

A careful selection of high usage but irregular words (such as *of* and *what*) are taught on code sheets and by showing the children how to make picture-coded spelling pictures.

A 'box' routine allows you to include any irregular, high interest words which you may need early on.

Sentence Awareness and Reading for Meaning

From the start you require meaningful responses from the children to short sentences on flashcards. They begin building sentences right after you have introduced the first six Letterland characters and a few flashcard words.

Terrington St. Clement Infants School, Kings Lynn, Norfolk.

Yeading Infants School, Hayes, Middx.

Development of Reading and Spelling Together

You foster early mastery of spelling by getting the children to construct words bodily (*3-D Word Making*), to construct them again on picture code cards, and then write the same words down.

You also use the tried and tested language-experience method; writing down the children's own language beneath their pictures for them to re-read and to copy. You picture code the occasional letter as a form of highlighting. This ensures that the children do not merely copy your writing unthinkingly.

Early Creative Writing

The imaginative range of Letterland gives children an opportunity to expand their own writing. They may, for example, transpose personal experience on to favourite characters and enjoy their involvement in the new role.

11

Your Teaching Materials

The following materials are supplied in your Letterland Starter Pack, along with this Teacher's Guide.

Scope and Sequence Charts

The charts list a growing vocabulary of words to read and write, showing where they occur in the teaching sequence and the various ways in which you may like to use them throughout the programme.

Wall Frieze

This frieze, in full colour, is divided into three sections so that you can display one third of it at a time, if you wish.

Display the frieze at a comfortable height so that the children can walk alongside it, talk about the letters together, finger-trace them with ease, and match the pictogram or plain letter sides of their Picture Code Cards.

> See also current catalogues for new products recently published.

Picture Code Cards

There are 50 Picture Code Cards, pictogram sides in colour. Plain black letters on reverse sides. For shape/sound recognition and word building.

Colour Stickers

Sheets of stickers of all the letters in the Pictogram Alphabet are provided in full colour for each child. They will serve numerous purposes: as an award or incentive in the course of learning the STEPS, and as headings for the childrens' own personal dictionaries.

Listen and Write Sheet Masters

Photocopy these sheets to give each child one per letter. Use at different age and ability levels. Instructions on page 148, The children may take home the Listen and Write Sheets, forming a valuable link between the parents and the school. See Parent Involvement, pages 31, 148, 149 and 152.

Code Sheet Masters

Each Code Sheet photocopy is intended to be used many times over by each child as described on page 149. The sheets can also be taken home, either for further practice or to show how many words have been mastered so far – another link to parents.

Songbook and Audio Tapes

Tape One introduces each letter's sound, provides 26 handwriting verses (spoken and sung), a Letterland theme song and 8 songs about vowels, **sh, wh, ing** and number **one** Simple percussion and recorder parts are provided. The 'Singsongs for A–Z' tape practises the **a–z** sounds to familiar tunes. See page 156–158.

Flashcards

In addition to the **a-z** Cards, you may find word flashcards supportive. Three or four of these are suggested in each Step. Instructions are on page 160 for making these cards. You may also like to make a Character Name Flashcard for each letter.

Consonant Capers Masters, Songs & Tape 2A Use the 'Consonant Capers' verses in any order. Select them one by one after the relevant Steps, or introduce them all after Step 26 for a focus on blending. See page 159.

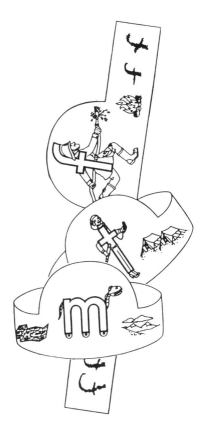

5 yr olds at Downsend Lodge School, Surrey

13

Your Instruction Language

The difficulties inherent in traditional phonic teaching lie in part in the language of instruction. Children have to learn it. They cannot speak it naturally, and they do not find it interesting.

Letterland introduces a story-like instruction language where phonic facts ride home on little analogies which children readily understand. The stories 'lift' your instruction, making it immediate for the children. From the very beginning they can speak this story language too. The chart below shows the shift in language. The changes, though small in detail, are far-reaching in effect.

Traditional Teacher's Language	Letterland Teacher's Language
● The teacher refers to each letter as 'it', and speaks about either 'the aee, the bee, and the cee' or 'the ah, the buh, and the cuh', etc.	● Each letter is 'he' or 'she', and both teacher and children speak about them by their character names, like talking about friends.
Disadvantages:	**Advantages:**
● Both 'aee, bee, cee' and 'ah, buh, cuh' are meaningless terms. No logic connects them to their letters.	● All 26 names are made from descriptive and meaningful words, so children can learn them as readily as friends' names.
● Alphabet names are treacherous. In 8 consonants the correct sound is at the start. In 6 it falls at the end, and in the remaining 7 at *neither* end! The five vowel names give no clue to the short vowel sounds. To add to the confusion 15 letters actually begin with *another* letter's sound (c, f, g, h, k, l, m, n, q, r, s, u, w, x, y)!	● The child *always* finds the correct sound just by starting to name the character.
	● Alliteration, built into each character name, reinforces the correct sound in every case.
● Position words are ambiguous: 'before', 'after', 'followed by', 'in front of', 'behind', 'to the right of the ...' etc.	● Every letter has an **unambiguous** front and back side, so all words describing position are clear from the start.
● Technical phrases are hard to follow: e.g. 'short' and 'long sounds' 'hard' and 'soft' sounds 'this is a consonant' 'this is a vowel' 'It says its name'	● Technical phrases avoided where possible: Not used Not used Not used 'He is a Vowel Man' 'He says his name'
● Digraphs are not logical: The teacher states a dry fact to rote learn – for example, **sh**: 'When you see 'ess' next to 'aitch' in a word the new sound will be 'sh'.' (No reason available.)	● Digraphs are made logical: The teacher tells a brief story – e.g. **sh**: 'When you see Sammy Snake next to the Hairy Hat Man he hushes Sammy Snake up like this, '**sh**!', because the Hairy Hat Man hates noise.
Children must suppress their first information about 'ess' and 'aitch' when learning the new sound.	Children use what they already know to understand a new development in an earlier story.

By adopting the language of Letterland, you are laying the foundations for teaching *all letter combinations* in the same story-telling style.

Eliciting Language from the Children

The use of Letterland to aid vocabulary expansion does not end with the stories which you teach. You encourage the children to build their own imagery around the characters and the place.

English is rich with adjectives. You help the children to decide which words apply to different characters. Is the Hairy Hat Man handsome? Helpful? Handy with his hands? Honest? Yes! Is he quick to quarrel? Ah no! Who is quick to quarrel? The Quarrelsome Queen, of course. What hobbies might the Hat Man have? The children can decide. They may suggest hopscotch, hide and seek, hang-gliding, even hunting for hedgehogs! You give them confidence to speak up by making them realise that it is their ideas that count. Where might Jumping Jim live? In a jigsaw house? He might! What would a jigsaw house look like? They decide. A child suggests that Bouncy Ben might live in a bouncing burrow! Again they decide. Original drawings often follow, together with an abundance of creative writing about Letterland and many other subjects.

English as a Second Language

By dispensing with the traditional alphabet names in the early stages of phonic instruction, the Letterland approach saves ESL children from having to cope with the bewildering feature that no less than seven of the alphabet names are also high-usage English words:

> *I, you, are, a, be, see* and *why*,
> not to mention
> *bee, sea, eye, oh, pea* and *tea*.

Somehow, the non-English speaker must quickly gather whether the teacher is using them as common words or terms for letters.

The Letterland character names enable ESL children to learn useful words: for example, **g** is Golden Girl in her garden swing. Before they know it, they have learnt six English words, the **g**-shape, and the **g**-sound as well. The alliterative Letterland names alone incorporate over forty common words.

While ESL children may not be able to keep up with the whole range of language activity contained in the first STEPS, they can share immediately in the play-acting, art, crafts and singing. Much of the story logic can be retold in their native language (a good opportunity for parent involvement). Meanwhile the Letterland characters mediate between the ESL children and the undeciphered letters, motivating them to master all the new shapes and sounds.

Children with Special Needs

It was children with special needs who, in the first instance, inspired the idea of Letterland stories to explain the behaviour of letters in words.

The fusing of a Pictogram into each letter has also been shown to help the more severely handicapped child, the partially-sighted, the partially-deaf, the neurologically and the motor-handicapped child. The system reaches them not just through their eyes, ears or hands but also by offering them a 'Letterland logic' to strengthen otherwise difficult rote learning. Because the facts acquire reasons they are easier to remember.

Kicking Race, Letterland Sports Day

Dealing with Difficult Words

'Letters'; 'Words'. Children frequently confuse the terms 'letter' and 'word' with each other, so do not take it for granted that they will immediately understand these abstract terms. You will make them familiar by talking about the letter people and animals who "love to get together to make words". At first, use the phrases "the Apple letter", "Bouncy Ben's letter", "Clever Cat's letter" etc, so the term 'letter' takes on meaning.

When the children are wearing *letters* they will be placing themselves bodily into sequences to create *words*. This will help the meaning of both these collective terms to become clear.

'Sounds'; 'Names'. These terms can also be confusing . Explain that every character in Letterland makes his or her special *sound*. Some letters make two sounds. The *only* characters who say their *names* in words are the five Vowel Men.

New Terms

'Vowel Man'; 'Vowel Men'; 'Mr'. Refer to each of the 'Vowel Men' by name: Mr A is a Vowel Man, so is Mr E, etc. The word 'vowel' needs no explanation at first (see pages 34 and 142).

'Reading Direction'. Each Pictogram acts as a signpost orientating the children's eyes in the 'Reading Direction' (to the right) through parallels to their own bodies and actions (jumping, kicking etc).

A word of warning! When you are facing the children make sure you do not point to *your* right. It is always safest to turn around, so that both you and the children are facing the same way whenever you are demonstrating the Reading Direction.

Most children find 'Reading Direction' an easy term to follow.

How to use this Book

The initial STEPS in this Teacher's Guide are set out in considerable detail. The later STEPS are set out more briefly, since by then you will have acquired confidence in the story-telling style of teaching Letterland and seen how it strengthens communication between you and your children.

Some sections are sign-posted *'Now or Later'*. These contain teaching of more advanced sounds which some children may be ready to learn. The choice of timing is left in your hands.

Three of these 'Now or Later' sections give the children a taste of the dynamic stage of word formation in which letters change their sounds (**sh, wh** and **-ng**). New stories explain the new sounds. The important feature in them is their logic. The storyline does not contradict the logic of the earlier stories, but extends it instead. These 'Now or Later' sections also give you a glimpse of the way Letterland logic operates in the Main Pack, so as to make more than 60 further letter combinations easy for children to understand, remember and enjoy.

Develop your Own Letterland Style

The STEPS are not intended to be taught word for word. Suggested teacher dialogue is printed in blue — if you feel it will help to read these out aloud until you are familiar with them, then do so. But your aim should be to find your own wording as soon as possible. Your eye contact with the children is more important. You will also feel freer to enjoy the spontaneity in your classroom which will spring from the mix of Letterland fact and fantasy.

The Pictogram System offers great flexibility. You can develop your own ideas and stories around the characters and encourage the children to contribute their own ideas. Letterland simply becomes a natural part of your language curriculum.

Whole Class or Small Groups ?

Either is acceptable. If your children are good listeners, class presentation is quicker. Use small groups and one-to-one teaching mainly to reinforce information from the stories. You may also wish to tell one of the more advanced stories to a particular child or group.

Pacing: How fast or slow?

Most teachers find that their reception class pupils comfortably learn all the **aA–zZ** shapes and sounds, and the correct handwriting strokes for **a–z**, within two or three months. Each STEP is intended to occupy one or two class sessions, work sheets included. Supportive art and craft work will take additional time.

Aim to introduce three or four letters a week. Feel free to proceed more slowly in the beginning, but do not be surprised if the children increase the pace for you by asking for more little stories – unaware perhaps that they are asking to learn more about reading and spelling.

St. Mary's C. of E. Infants School, Cumbria.

Whitehouse Common Infants School, Birmingham.

Springmead J.M.I. School, Herts.

18

Longford Infants, Staffs.

Garfield Primary School, Bradford, Yorks.

TEACHING ROUTINES

Each of the following routines is set out for you in detail where it first occurs in a STEP. Subsequently, most of these routines are referred to simply by their logos, to act as reminders for you. They are listed again on page 24 with stars to indicate their importance for different age groups.

Picture Coding   Adding Pictogram details to each letter. This routine is important. Your pupils become the animators of the lifeless letters. The drawing process is fun. It also greatly increases attention to the shape, sound and orientation of each letter.

Both you and the children will be animating specific letters on flashcards, children's names, artwork and worksheet work throughout the STEPS. You use this special animating process only as long as the children need its support. By the time the novelty of drawing heads, feet etc, on the letters has worn off, the picture coding will have served its purpose.

Boxes   You draw a box around certain words or letters to signal that they are irregular. It indicates to the children that they should regard the word in it as a whole-word shape. The box also tells children to ask you about the word if they cannot read it. While you keep irregular words to a minimum at first, the box routine allows you to bring in any high interest words you may need.

Trace   Air tracing, tracing on windows, in sand, etc, and on the Picture Code Cards can be valuable for writing beginners. Older children probably will not need this tactile reinforcement.

Repeat Handwriting Verse   While the children trace, they say or sing little verses describing the stroke they are making. Parents can help in learning the verses and practising handwriting at home.

Sing   The Letterland characters offer many opportunities for singing. Use the 'Singsong for Letter Sounds' section on page 156 both as a vehicle for practising the **a – z** sounds and for recreation.

Play-act   Play-acting takes the animation of the letters further. Now the children become the characters, play-acting their shapes and sounds. Such acting gives the child kinaesthetic experience to link to each letter. You may like to add props, since dressing up transforms work into play in the children's minds.

Quick Dash for Letters   This is a review of the Picture Code cards learnt so far. You first flash each Pictogram card and the children respond with the character's name. You flash each card again and they give you the letter's sound.

Quick Dash for Words   Use the character name flashcards. Show the picture-coded side first; then the plain side. In due course flash the plain sides only.

Merland Rise First School, Surrey.

19

3-D Word Making   Detachable letters are worn/held by children. (Stick these on to headbands, tabards, etc.) With your help the children sequence themselves in the correct order to make up a word. This activity gives you valuable opportunities to discuss letter sounds, to work on blending sounds and, later, to talk about silent or interacting letters *right where they occur* in a particular word.

3-D Word Copying   With three children standing in sequence, the rest of the children copy the word from their standing friends. This is a very effective way to start on learning to spell.

Word Building with Picture Code Cards   Any Pictogram on these cards can be added or taken away from a word by a flick of the wrist. The Pictogram sides enable the children to 'see' the sounds and to appreciate letter sequence. At the same time the plain letters are right to hand as soon as the children are ready to graduate to them.

Flashcard Sentence Building   The Scope and Sequence Charts show you the range of sentences which the children can quickly make.

Action Sentences   These give practice in silent reading. By their actions the children show they have understood the sentences. Many are listed on the Scope and Sequence Charts.

Spelling Pictures   Spelling pictures provide an opportunity to picture code some or all letters of a word, and illustrate the whole word's meaning.
The children thus confirm the phonic and the whole word properties of a chosen word, *both within one picture.* Useful words for this routine are listed in Scope and Sequence Chart No.1.

Slow-Speak Spelling   In this routine you occasionally slow down your voice in order to emphasise each sound in a short word. For example, "Do you think the Hairy Hat Man is a nice *mmmannn*?" (Do not pause: muh/..a/..muh.)

Encourage the children to use the slow-speak routine as necessary and let it lead to spelling out the slow-speak word, either in 3-D, using the Picture Code Cards or on paper. Your aim is to ensure that the children realise that they are *capturing live speech*, and that writing, in fact, is a way of keeping words after the talking is over.

Gamlingay Primary School, Cambs.

Good slow-speak words are those which you can pronounce *slowly and continuously* without distortion of their sound. Many are underlined on the Scope and Sequence Chart. Use them for helping children to spell by ear.

Listen and Write Sheets   Instructions for ways of using these sheets are given on page 148.

Code Sheets   Special points to note for each sheet are given within the relevant STEP. General instructions on page 149.

Sing   Use the 'Singsong for Letter Sounds' (page 156) both for practising the a–z sounds and for recreation. The 'Singsong' Tape gives the tunes and precise pronunciation. Extra tapes to lend to parents will ensure they do not mispronounce **a–z**.

Parent Involvement   The house logo indicates points in the STEPS when you may like to enlist parents' support at home.

Consonant Capers   Suggestions for use on page 158.

The Teaching Order
c, a, d, h, m, t, s, i, n, y, g, o, f, p, k, e, l, v, w, j, b, u, qu, r, x, z.
The STEPS begin with **c, a** and **d** to reinforce the circle and stick handwriting movements. They then shift to **h, m** and **t** to keep interest high and to allow the children to group letters into meaningful words early on. The rest of the STEP order is designed to keep potentially confusing letter shapes well apart (**d/b/p/q, n/u, m/w, s/z**, etc), to introduce the vowels **a** and **i** first (because they occur in many essential words) and steadily to increase the number of words the children might sound out, spell and *read for meaning*.

Both the Listen and Write Sheets and the Code Sheets are designed to reinforce the STEP order. Alternatively, the Listen and Write Sheets can be completed first if special teaching circumstances require it.

Proceed with further handwriting practice in conjunction with any good programme such as New Nelson's Handwriting or C. Jarman's Development of Handwriting Skills, Blackwell.

Capital Letters
Since Pictograms make the link between lower case and capital letters easy to learn, there is no need, for example, to write days of the week like this: **monday** or **tuesday** or to limit early reading to sentences with no capital letters. Instead, you can let the children see words from the outset just as they appear in the world outside the classroom. Simply add the picture code to confirm the link: **Monday** and **Tuesday**.

monday   **Monday**

tuesday   **Tuesday**

Children's Names
Children's names provide excellent teaching opportunities because they greatly enjoy discovering 'who' from Letterland helps them to spell their name. Names, however, often contain silent letters and exceptions. So, when you picture code the children's names for them, simply signpost any silent letter by using grey-coloured paint, or by writing it in dotted lines. Box any letters which make an unusual sound to warn the child. In some cases you can promise an explanatory story later. You might also box any digraphs which will come later in the term.

See examples on inside back cover.

Section 2

Now you are ready to start introducing the Letterland characters in earnest, and discussing their role in words. Symbols refer to teaching routines described in Section 1. For further details, see page 24.

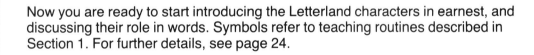

Preparing for the Steps

Setting the Scene

You may like to begin your teaching with a short 'Going to Letterland' routine which can be used whenever you wish before sessions. For example, let the children join hands and set off round the room singing "This is the way to Letterland". (The words and tune are on page 156).

Or, all pretend to climb onto a magic Letterland carpet, flying on it to the special place called Letterland where all the letter people and alphabet animals live.

Or, you and the children ask each other "How do you get to Letterland?" Then answer each other with "Just open a book!" One of you slowly and dramatically opens a book, with large print, and peers into it. To leave Letterland you ceremoniously close the book.

Later, you can ask the children to invent new ways of getting to Letterland. Adapt your routine to incorporate their ideas and foster language enrichment.

Logos for Teaching Routines

Familiarise yourself with the logos, set out below, together with the page number on which they first occur. Look through the STEPS and see how they recur regularly as signposts, indicating where you may wish to include the relevant teaching routine.

Remember to develop your own presentation of the letters as the scheme progresses. Use your own judgement to decide how much to make use of each routine when signposted. You may wish to use all of them with very young pupils. Slightly older children may need only the starred routines. Wherever the words 'Scope and Sequence Chart' occur, see both Chart No. 1 and 2.

Flashcards, Murals, Picture Code Cards and Props

Check that you have the appropriate materials before commencing each STEP by reading the preparation panels, marked with a ⓟ, at the beginning of each STEP.

A mural is suggested to launch the first three STEPS. Make it in three parts, like the one below. Mount it at a convenient height on the wall so the children can easily add their own work to it. Encourage the children to use the mural, sticking on and taking off cats (see STEP 1) and, later, apples and ducks (STEPS 2 and 3). You can use this exercise not only for teaching sounds, but for counting activities as well. (Add **b's** later.)

Hold your Picture Code Cards up so no fingers hide any part of the letter. The palm of your hand will also cut out any light which might otherwise show through from behind.

Headbands   At first you will need to make only three. (See the instructions on page 160.) Alternatively you can purchase 32 Letterland headbands as illustrated on page 22 for the children to colour. The set includes 5 long vowel headbands and Oscar's Little Brother (irregular o in come, love, brother, etc.).

Make Arrows   Let the children make paper arrows pointing to the right, to mount on each of the classroom walls. Put signs saying 'Reading Direction' over them. The children need not understand the Reading Direction concept immediately, but it will become valuable as your teaching progresses.

Letterland ABC and 20 Storybooks   (with audio tapes)   All these titles bring alive the imaginary place called Letterland. The stories turn on alliterative words, making valuable listening experiences before children are able to read them independently. Later on they feel proud when they can.

Letterland Links   There are currently 40 titles in this series. Each one provides both entertainment and consolidation of the shape and sound of one letter or more. Use these little books as 'read to', 'read with', 'sing with', or 'read alone' texts.

Clever Cat

You are beginning with the letters **c**, **a** and **d** in your first three STEPS for several reasons.
1. All three letters reinforce one basic handwriting movement.
2. Two of them (**d** and **a**) allow you and the children to create two useful words ('dad' and 'add') even before you teach any more of the alphabet (see *3-D Word Making*, page 42).
3. The characters of Clever Cat, Annie Apple and Dippy Duck lend themselves well to art and craft activities from the start.

(P) Mural and Flashcards

Your 'journey' to Letterland can begin with the working mural, setting the scene with a cat's picnic. Prepare flashcards for the words shown on the right, following the instruction page 160.

Mount the centre section of your mural – a picnic scene with green surroundings (see page 25) – at an accessible height on a wall, with room to add a panel on each side later, if possible.

Prepare plain, thick black **c**-shapes on pieces of card which each child will animate and take home. Prepare six or seven extra ones in varying sizes for use with the mural. Back them with blu-tak or another similar material which will make them easily detachable.

The Shift to Letterland Names

Some children are bound to come to school already knowing some of the traditional alphabet. Because many of these terms are misleading, explain how *you* will be talking about the letters roughly as follows.

Some of you may be used to calling these letters by the names 'aee', 'bee' and 'cee'. (Show plain sides of the cards.) Those are alphabet names. Your mothers and fathers may talk about them that way too.

But the Letterland people and animals you see on these cards (show picture sides) don't call each other by their alphabet names. They call each other by their Letterland names instead, names like Annie Apple, Bouncy Ben* and Clever Cat . .**

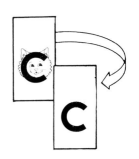

Meet Clever Cat

Show the Pictogram side of the Picture Code Card **c**.

First of all, let me tell you something about this letter. *She* is called Clever Cat and she lives in Letterland. Most of the time you can't see Clever Cat's face in her letter because she likes to keep it a secret that she's there. Luckily on this card you *can* see her face – some of the time!

Turn the card to the plain side, then back to the Pictogram side.

But even on this side her face is all you can see. So you will just have to pretend you can see her body and tail as well.

You are going to make some pictures of Clever Cat's face, just like this one. Let's see you add her ears and her eyes and her whiskers so it looks like the Clever Cat on my card.

Hand out your plain **c** shapes and crayons (yellow for fur, pink for nose and inner ears).

This will be the children's first experience of picture coding. If their motor control is poor, add a cat's face yourself first. Then give duplicates so all they need to do is add colour.

Let the children take their time. While they are animating the abstract letter shape they are forging an indelible link between the symbol and its sound.

Encourage them to talk about Clever Cat, telling you what they are doing as they colour in her ears, eyes, nose and fur. Let them talk about any cats they own or about pets in general.

*The letter **b** is introduced much later in this Starter Pack to keep the letters **b** and **d** well apart. Do not let this fact prevent you from answering any child who asks 'who' **b** is. The aim is not to withhold the letter's identity but only to postpone your in-depth focus on it.

** The flashcards illustrated in this Guide are stencilled for clarity. You may prefer to use the pre-cursive style letter formation as set out in the 'Towards Cursive' Letterland Handwriting Programme Stages One and Two, now available, which includes short exit strokes on **a,d,h,i,k,l,m, n,t** and **u**, and the curved **y** shape.

Clever Cat's Sound

What sounds do most cats make? (Elicit 'meeow' sound and purring.) That's right, but Clever Cat is just not like other cats. *She* makes a different, special sound instead. She doesn't even say it loudly. She *whispers* it, like this '**c..,c..,c...**'

Can you make Clever Cat sound, '**c..,c..,c...**'?

The room should be filled with whispered '**c...**' sounds. Make sure the children notice their own throat sounds by cupping their hands around their necks. Make sure also that they do not distort the '**c...**' sound into '**cuh**'. This is very important for later reading.

What a lovely lot of Clever Cats you are!

Choose children to stick the extra cats on the mural. Put the smaller ones on the far side of the picnic cloth.

After this lesson seize any natural opportunity that arises (e.g. *custard* at lunch) to comment on hearing Clever Cat's '**c...**' sound at the beginning of words.

Clever Cat's Letter Shape

Lead up to writing **c** by explaining roughly as follows:

Some animals love it when you stroke them gently. Clever Cat likes you to stroke her, as long as you do it very smoothly and carefully, exactly the way she likes it. Here's a little poem which tells you how she wants you to stroke her:

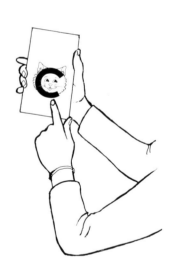

> Curve round Clever Cat's
> face to begin.
>
> Then gently tickle her
> under her chin.

All 26 handwriting verses are set out on pages 152-155, together with suggestions for parent involvement. These verses can also be chanted to music on Letterland Audio Tape No. 1.

Let some children finger trace the Pictogram side of the card, others trace the **c** shape in the air, on the board, or perhaps on the window as they repeat the verse.

Turn to the plain **c** side of your card.

Now let's all stroke Clever Cat again, but this time we will only see her *letter, without* her face.

Encourage the children to go on 'seeing' Clever Cat's face by imagining that it is still there, within her letter. (This is a good visual memory training exercise, so get the children to practise it with each new letter.)

Clever Cat in Words: cat, cats

Have your **cat** and **cats** flashcards ready. Then recap as follows before you introduce them.

Let's think about what we have done so far.
- We met Clever Cat. (Discuss.)
- We *coloured* in Clever Cat. (What *colours*?)
- We *cupped* our hands around our throats to feel the way Clever Cat makes her little '**c...**' sound. (All make her sound.)
- We *cut* out the Clever Cats.
- We stuck some Clever Cats on our big picture.
- We learned how Clever Cat likes to be stroked. (Repeat the verse and stroke **c** in the air.)

Show the **cat** flashcard.

Clever Cat has found two other letters (point to them) to help her make this word. Of course the word she likes to make best is **cat** because she *is* a cat. So here she is, making her little '**c...**' sound at the beginning of the word **cat**. I'm going to *whisper* the word **cat** (point) and I want you to listen for her '**c...**' sound at the beginning of the word:

ca...t, ca..t, cat.

(Be careful not to distort the word by pausing after **c**.)

Tell them that the word on your next card says **cats**, so you are going to put it with the cats on the mural.

Compare Small c and Capital C

Many children come to school having been taught capital letters at home, whereas you will wish to limit capitals to the beginning of their names in their early writing. At the STEP 3 stage you will be introducing the first sections of your small and capital letter frieze. In the meantime, explain the difference between small and capital **C** as follows.

One exciting thing about Letterland animals is that they can change size whenever they want to. All they have to do is take a deep breath and they become bigger. Wouldn't if be fun if you and I could do that too?

Allow discussion.

This getting bigger trick is how Letterland animals and people like to show us that they are starting an important word. Names are important, so you will always see them looking bigger than the other letters at the beginning of a name.

Introduce the **Clever Cat** flashcard to draw attention to the capital **C**'s. You introduce the **cats picnic** flashcard with three small **c**'s for comparison, and to use afterwards as a further label for the mural.

Treat all character names as sight words from the start. Aim at this point to develop a habit of looking for recurring capital letters in two successive words. This will occur in every Letterland character's name.

Now you know that Clever Cat loves being in words. She just loves making her clever little 'c...' sounds in them.

What's more, Clever Cat can be in several places at the same time! Being in more than one place at a time is another special thing which only Letterland people and animals can do. Look, here's Clever Cat in three different places in these words (**cats picnic**), and two different places in these words (**Clever Cat**).

The two words on this card are Clever Cat's own name. They say 'Clever Cat'. These other two words say 'cats picnic'.

You can tell which card has Clever Cat's name on it because *she* knows names are important. So she takes a deep breath and makes herself bigger, twice, on this card.

Mix cards behind your back.

So which card has Clever Cat's name on it? Yes! The one where she looks bigger, because she is starting her name, Clever Cat.

Write Clever Cat's Letter

Let's pretend you have Clever Cat in front of you. Let's stroke around her head the way she likes it.

Emphasise the gross motor movement at this stage, involving the whole arm. Repeat the verse at the same time.

Listen and Write Sheet 1: c

Hand out photocopies. Discuss the pictures and **c**-sounds. Have the children discover the odd one out, and colour all pictures *except* this odd one. Use the lower half as suggested on page 148.

Parent Involvement

At the end of the day the children can take the Listen and Write Sheets home, together with a copy of the **c** handwriting verse, photocopied and guillotined into a strip from page 152, so that parents can support handwriting practice and verse learning at home.

Clever Cat Song

Hold up your **c** card, showing the Pictogram side, while everyone sings the first verse of the Clever Cat song on page 156.

Play Acting: Be Clever Cat

Let the children all pretend to be cats. They can creep, crawl, climb, claw imaginary carpets, and catch imaginary caterpillars. They can play a Copy Cat game ('Clever Cat says do this...' instead of 'Simon says...').

Clever Cat in Names

Take advantage of capital **C** shapes in children's names. If there is a Carol, Claire, Catherine or Carl, etc, in the class, point out how Clever Cat loves taking a deep breath and becoming bigger to show how important she feels when she can make her '**c...**' sound at the beginning of *their* names, just as she does in her own!

Write any appropriate children's names in bold black paint and let their owners code Clever Cat's face. Then display their efforts on the wall. Point out the **C**'s from time to time as Claire's Clever Cat and Carl's Clever Cat, etc.

Exceptions: The Other Sounds of c

What about the children in your class called Cecilia, Cherry, Charles, Charlotte, Cynthia or any other name which does *not* begin with a hard **c** sound?

At this stage for simplicity's sake, let these children add the cat's face as usual. Then put a box around these **c**'s.

Explain that the box means that you have a special little story about them which you will tell later. It will explain why Clever Cat is making a *different sound* in their name. (*See also Boxes, page 19, 150, 160.*)

Clever Cat Everywhere!

Hopefully the children will also now start to spot the **c** shape in words about the school, and outside. Remind them that Clever Cat can be in lots of places at the same time, so they should be on the look out everywhere. They may spot her on signs, cars, cereal packets, etc.

This is also a good time to put up picture-coded labels wherever an object beginning with the hard **c** sound gives you the opportunity.

Code Sheet 1: cC

Hand out copies of this code sheet and follow the general instructions on page 149. Let the children make Letterland folders which will eventually hold all their Code Sheets. These Code Sheets will be used many times, not only to study letter behaviour after each STEP, but also to provide important reading practice and revison of previous STEPS.

Oral curled up comfortable can climb claws
curve cosy cushion could cling clever

Picture Coding Avoid smudging by having the children colour in yellow cat's fur before overwriting the broken-line **c**'s in red or black.

First Dictionary

Award to each child a **c** sticker for learning all about Clever Cat. Place it on page 3 of an exercise book which will become their own personal first dictionary. (Number all the pages for quick placement of later stickers.) Complete beginners may like to write one row of small **c**'s now directly under their sticker, or wait until they have learnt to write enough letters to enter their first word (**cat**, after STEP 6: **tT**). Older children may like to enter the Code Sheet vocabulary **cats, clever** and **caterpillar** now.

Costume Box

Now is a good time to start a costume box specifically for Letterland props. You might like to call it Clever Cat's Costume Box, and picture code the capital C's to highlight the alliterative words.

The Next Steps

Remember that, for the sake of brevity, teaching routines will now often be referred to by symbols. These will remind you of your options. Be prepared to skip any routine you judge unnecessary. For some groups of children less consolidation is needed, while others will benefit best from using them all.

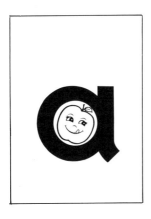

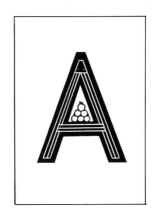

Annie Apple, the Applestand & Mr A

You will now be introducing two new shapes, **a** and **A**, and the **short a** sound. You will also be talking, but only casually, about **Mr A** as the owner of the apples, in anticipation of teaching the **long a** sound.

(P) Mural and Flashcards

Make a background for the left-hand section of your existing mural (see page 25). Paint the trees so that the children can add a few of their own hand-coloured apples. The apples should be detachable.

Prepare whole word flashcards for the words on the right. Picture code the **a**'s on one side only. Keep all other letters on both sides *plain*.

Draw and duplicate enough **a**'s for the children to picture code and take home, and enough extra ones to fill the trees.

Make an **A**-shaped paper applestand which can be added to the mural later.

Annie Apple
add an apple
Take it away, Mr A
add 2 apples
add 3 apples

The Apple Letter Shape and Sound

Point to an apple tree on the mural.

This is **an a**pple tree growing in Letterland. We are going to help it to grow lots of apples.

Distribute duplicated **a**'s and let the children draw and colour red apples inside them. Let them add faces on them if they wish. While they colour, explain as follows.

Now don't forget that all these apples which you are making (hold up the Pictogram side of your card) are *Letterland* apples, growing inside a letter – this apple letter shape. (Turn to plain side of card.)

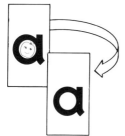

Letterland apples are, oh, so special. Not all of them are eating apples. Some of them are *talking* apples, like the one here called Annie Apple.

Let's pretend you have a real, very big apple in front of you and you are about to take a big bite. At the same time you start to say 'apple', like this 'ă...'!

All mime biting an apple and saying 'ă'.

That is exactly what Annie Apple and all the other talking apples say. They say 'ă...'! Whoever heard of apples that can say 'ă'? It *is* rather fantastic, and it can only happen in Letterland!

The apples which you are making here are all *talking* apples. While you finish colouring in your talking apples let's hear all of you talk like Letterland apples. Say 'ă...ă...ă...', like that.

Choose several children.

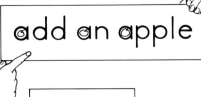

Now let's see each of you come in turn and *add an apple* to the trees. (Point to your **add an apple** flashcard as you speak.)

As you do this let's hear you say 'ă...ă...ă...' again, just like a real Letterland apple.

When all the apples have been added to the trees, compare the flashcards and let the children decide that **apples** is the best one to put on the mural to label so many apples.

Preparation for Long Vowels

While you will continue to stress 'the apple sound' in words, talk briefly now about Mr A (from Asia). Describe Mr A as a 'Vowel Man' and as 'the owner of the apples'. No explanation of the term 'vowel' is needed at this stage. Just let the children become used to hearing the word. (See also Note, page 85)

1

All these apples in Letterland belong to a Vowel Man called Mr A. You can tell that his talking apples must be very special because Mr A has come from a far away place called Asia, especially to grow these apples and look after them.

Show Pictogram side of your Mr A card.

2

Mr A collects all his apples in his apron. That is why everyone calls him 'Mr A, the Apron Man'.

Mr A sells lots of *eating* apples in his shop but he puts the special *talking* apples into words which need an 'ă' sound in them.

Write the Apple Letter

Air trace the correct stroke, supporting it with the Annie Apple handwriting verse below. (Music is available on Letterland Audio Tape No. 1.)

> At the leaf begin.
> Go *round* the apple this way.
>
> Then *add* a line *down*,
> so Annie won't roll away.

Remember that all the handwriting verses are set out in larger print on page 152, so that you can send home a photocopy in a size of print the children will eventually be able to read.

Listen and Write Sheet 2. Hand out photocopies and use as instructed on page 148, including parent involvement if possible.

Capital A (Short Sound)

Explain the capital **A** shape as follows.

Mr A likes to make neat little Applestands for his talking apples. You can often see these Applestands at the beginning of words. (Find a few capital **A**'s in a large print book.)

Add your Applestand to the mural.

You will also see these Applestands at the beginning of names which Mr A has given to his talking apples, names like: Annie Apple, Andy Apple, Alison Apple and Adam Apple.

Show your **Annie Apple** flashcard.

Here is Annie Apple's name and here is Annie Apple herself, right in the middle of the Applestand!

Apple Song

See page 156. Sing this verse to the tune of *'Here we go round the Mulberry Bush'*. At the same time, have the children bob up and down like apples on a branch.

While they sing, hold up your apple card. Have the Mr A card hidden behind it until the last line. Then place the Mr A card at the front. Let the children point to it as they sing the last line.

Applestands in Names

Help any children whose names begin with a short **a** sound to discover the Applestands in their names, e.g. Alan, Annette, and code them with <u>one</u> apple, Annie, who takes a deep breath and gets bigger because names are important. Display these children's name paintings. Remember to box letters in names that have irregular **a**'s, e.g. Arthur, Mary, and promise stories later to explain most of them.

Code Sheet 2: aA

Follow the general instructions on page 149.

Oral   appetite   Annie Apple   happy/sad   smiling
        appetising   could an ant...? cross/angry frowning

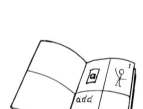

Picture Coding   Accept a picture of Annie Apple's face if the children spontaneously add it, but a red blotch is preferable for simplicity and speed.

Revision   Re-read **cC** sheet. Discover each apple letter. Listen and code them. Re-read again. Both **c**'s and **a**'s will now be prominent.

First Dictionary

Award to each child an **a** sticker for learning all about Annie Apple. After the next STEP they can add their first word: **add**. Later they can draw a stick man on the right and add the word **apron**.

Mr A in Words

Time this information to suit your children's ability. Make sure they are confident of Annie Apple's sound first.

Mr A is a very busy man but he loves being in words. So when he finds time you will hear him saying his name 'Ā!' loud and clear.

Can you hear Mr A saying his name right at the beginning of the word *apron*? (Make and show an **apron** flashcard.) You say it: āpron, ā-pron, āpron.

At this point pick out any children with a long **a** in their names: Jane, Nathan, etc.

Show them how to draw a stick man right through their apple letters to signal Mr A's presence. Display their names as paintings and treat them as special because Mr A always manages to find time to appear in them, even though he is such a busy man!

Mr A in the Word 'ā'

It is useful from the start to draw attention to Mr A's presence in one of the 12 most used words in the English language: **a**.

When we speak, we tend to pronounce this word as 'uh'. But to write it, a child must think 'ā', not 'u'. So now (or later if you are teaching complete beginners or children with special needs), it is a good idea to introduce a stick man into the word **a** in some phrases and sentences. This will accustom children to seeing two alternative picture codings for this one letter. It will also make their early writing free from contradiction over the sound of this extremely high-usage word.

By using a stick man to code the word **a**, you also prepare the way for the concept that every Vowel Man regularly appears in a few much used *little* words to say his name (Mr E in **be, he, she, we, me**; Mr I in **I**; Mr O in **go, so, no**; and Mr U at the end **you**).

Qasim has a canary.

Apple and Apron Game

Elect one child to wear an apron and be Mr A. Each child takes an apple off the mural and sits down with it. You hold up either the **add an apple** flashcard or the **Take it away, Mr A** flashcard. Each time, name a child who must stick his or her apple back on the tree or put it in Mr A's apron depending on which flashcard you hold up.

Vary the game by letting the children hold up the flashcards. You may also like to add further flashcards: **add 2 apples, add 3 apples**, etc, to contribute to counting activities.

Code Sheet 27: Mr A

Oral	belong to (own)	Vowel Man (owner)	Annie Apple's sound
	belong together	Mr A's belongings	Mr A's name

Each Vowel Man Code Sheet lists a few long vowel words. They are all high-usage words and therefore good ones to learn how to read and to code correctly first.

The children should take a decision: 'apple?' or 'Mr A himself?', as they are about to code each word.

In the top section they will need an apple in **ăm**. All the other **a**'s will need stick men. In the Main Pack more coding strategies will help children to PREDICT the value of ANY vowel in ANY unknown word. The apple/stick man strategy is simply strategy number one. The box routine keeps exceptions aside while you teach more strategies.

My baby has a big ball.

Dippy Duck
& the Duck Door

With the introduction of letter **d** you can give the children four new words to treat as sight words: **duck, ducks, Dippy Duck,** and two words based on sounds which they now know: **dad, add.** The latter two words are worthy of considerable attention as they will be the children's first experience of spelling, *and* their first discovery of meaning by miming letters and setting themselves up as a word (page 42).

Take care to refer to Dippy Duck as *she* when you show the children how to picture code her. Later, when you compare the **d** and **b** shapes you will find it useful to talk about *her* and *him* (Bouncy Ben), so that even your pronouns help to make your instructions totally clear.

Ⓟ Mural and Flashcards

Complete your wall mural by adding the part showing the pond (see page 25). The children will later add ducks to join the cats and apples already there. The completed mural can later be used for revision, discussion and counting activities.

Make and have ready the flashcards for the words shown on the right below.

Make enough plain **d**'s for the children to picture code and take home, and about seven more in varying sizes to place on the pond and diving board in the mural.

Since **dad** and **add** need two **d**'s, use your second **d** card in a further headband. (Later the children may like to decorate their own headbands to keep in the costume box for use in play time).

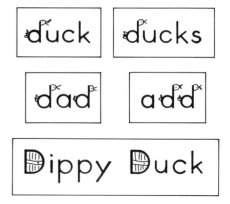

Dippy Duck's Shape and Sound

Meet Dippy Duck. She is quite a young duck, so she is covered with yellow down. (Discuss what *down* is; the pre-feather stage.)

What kind of sound does Dippy Duck make? Well, remember *she* is a Letterland duck, so *she* doesn't quack like other ducks you may have heard. She makes the sound that you can hear at the beginning of her name instead. If you start to say 'Dippy' *you* can make her sound too. It's like this: '**d..,d..,d...**'.

Make sure you clip your voice immediately following this sound. (It must not sound like 'duh', making blending difficult later. Keeping your mouth nearly shut helps.)

Focus now on the **d** shape by letting the children picture code their **d**'s in colour, and cut them out.

Write Dippy Duck's Letter

This is how Dippy Duck likes you to stroke her.

Air
Trace

Handwriting
Verse

Listen and
Write Sheet 3

Involve
Parents

Duckpond Mural

Select children to stick the detachable ducks onto the pond part of the mural. Talk about the following: **in the distance, near, nearer, nearest, big, bigger, biggest, small, smaller, smallest,** and **Dippy Duck's door** in the distance.

Duck Hunt

Beforehand, add picture coding to a few signs around the school. Then take the children on a walk, each of you whispering: "Do I see Dippy Duck in the distance?" as you search the hall, notices etc, for **d**'s and **D**'s, both picture coded and plain ones.

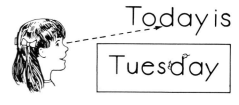

Dippy Duck and the Reading Direction

Use Dippy Duck's rightward orientation as a model for the children's eyes. Like her, they should always look ahead as they read.

Dippy Duck always swims in the Reading Direction in words (point to your sign and arrows on the wall), because in Letterland it is very important to know who is going to be next to you in a word. That is why she always looks ahead as she swims along.

It is a phonic fact that if a letter changes its sound it is because of the letter(s) next to it (e.g. **d** becomes silent because it is next to **ge** in **edge, bridge** etc). Predicting these changes is covered later. Meanwhile stress that Dippy Duck *never* turns around. She feels that if she *did* something *dreadful* would happen!

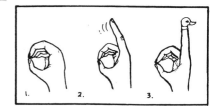

A Duck in Hand

You can bring Dippy Duck literally to hand for every child by explaining how to turn their *right* hands into Dippy Duck.

Put all the fingers of your right hand on your thumb. Then lift up your first finger. Imagine Dippy Duck's head on it, and you will see Dippy Duck's letter, right there in your hand!

Trace this paper duck head and duplicate it on stiff card. Let the children take their paper ducks home to colour. The duck's head is small so it is best if a parent cuts it out, bends and fixes it so that it will fit onto the child's right index finger for them to wear at school the next day.

Have all the class practise moving their index fingers so that Dippy Duck puts her head under her wing, then makes her head pop up again. Let them call this their 'duck hand'. It will always be there to remind them of Dippy Duck's shape, and will be especially useful later when you introduce **b, p** and **q.**

Song and Actions for Dippy Duck

Sing the duck song on page 156. Again, guard against a distorting 'uh' sound creeping in while singing: Add miming gestures – waddle, wing flapping etc. Also, have the children trace each other, life size, in waddle position.

Wall Frieze aA – eE

Display the first four letters of the wall frieze, folding **eE – hH** out of sight. Alternatively, mount the **aA – hH** sections in full now. Tell the children the names of the other characters if they ask, and promise stories about them later.

40

Capital D

Although you will avoid writing capital **D** at this stage, you will be talking about it in some detail. Let the children look at the **D** shape on the frieze and point out how straight one side of Dippy Duck's door is. Show how the door opens in the reading direction.

Make the children's name paintings beginning with **D** for them to picture code, e.g. David, Dora, Daniel, Debbie, and then display them in the classroom.

Now is a good time to picture code the capital **D** on your Reading Direction sign, and colour it yellow, while all the children watch you.

To make sure everyone understands that the capital **D** shape also stands for the **d...** sound, draw Dippy's head peeping out.

First   Later

Explain she is making her usual **d...** sound from just inside her front door.

Soon you can ask the children to just imagine her there.

Use your **Dippy Duck** and **duck** flashcards to explain that the meaning of the word **duck** is the same as **Duck**. Then put your **ducks** flashcard among the ducks on the mural to label them.

Moveable Dippy Duck Display

Have the children help you to make a duck and door collage. Make duck down from cotton wool dusted with dry yellow powder paint and simulate strips of wood for the duck door. Display the collage on a right-hand part of a wall. Ideally, make the duck moveable so the children can interact with it.

Let the display become a collecting place for words and objects beginning with **d**.

Costume Box

Add any spare yellow clothing (for cats and downy ducks) to your costume box. By now it should contain cat masks, apple leaf collars, aprons, etc, since this box is likely to be used in spontaneous play as well as for 3-D word making described on page 20.

First 3-D Words

Your children should now be ready to create their first word!

If the term 'letter' was meaningless at first, it will have more meaning now because they have play acted being letters themselves. Next, by grouping together, they will gain first-hand experience of being a 'word'.

Constructing a word in three dimensions like this is useful for your class, and especially helpful for any child who is educationally 'at risk'. You will be taking the words off the written page and into real life with them.

(P) Arrows and Headbands

Prepare arrows to stick on the floor pointing out out the Reading Direction. This will help the children when they are standing in a row to make a word.

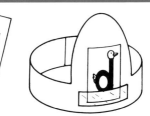

Slip your **a** and **d** picture code cards into the headbands already prepared page 160, or ones shown on page 22.

First Blending

Lead into blending **d** with **a** by introducing a 'Letterland secret' shared by all the consonants. Let the children chant or sing the following verse, (you can find the tune on Letterland Audio Tape No.1). Present this blending verse right now as 'Dippy Duck's secret'.

Blending verse

> I always sound better
> beside another letter,
> so don't make my sound
> all alone.
>
> Put a nice round apple
> right beside me,
> so I don't have to be
> on my own.

This 'secret' is especially useful for blends with **b, d, g** and **r**. (See also page 54, the 'store up and release' technique.)

Create 'dad'

Give headbands to two girls so that they become Annie Apple and Dippy Duck. Appoint a third child (boy or girl) to become 'Davey Duck', 'Dora Duck' or whatever name they choose. Place the three children on the class's left, with a wall as background.

Now Dippy Duck, let's see you swim along in the Reading Direction until you reach me. Say '**d..,d..,d..**' as you come, because '**d..**' is your sound. (Keep your mouth almost shut to avoid 'duh'.(Position this child in the centre.)

Can everyone see Dippy Duck here? Now I want you to think of this wall behind Dippy Duck as a great, big, white page in a book. Dippy Duck has just walked on to that page.

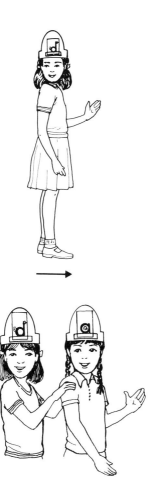

Make sure the child stands with his or her feet still pointing to the right while looking towards the class.

Remember Dippy Duck's secret. She doesn't like to make her sound all alone, does she? No. So let's give her an apple for company. Come on, Annie Apple. Say '**ă.., ă.., ă...**' as you come over to join Dippy.

Show her where to stand to make **da** .

Let's say Dippy Duck and Annie Apple's sound together now: '**dă...**'! Do any of you have a baby brother or sister who can't really talk yet but who can say '**dă**' or '**dă-dă**'?

Allow discussion of baby talk. Lead on to how older children call their fathers, *Daddy*, and maybe *Dad* for short.

You can say '**dad**' *easily*, can't you! Say '**dad**'. Say it again very slowly, '**dă...d**'. Did I hear you make a '**d**' sound at the *end* – '**dă...d**' – as well as at the beginning? Listen: **da...d**!

Davey Duck, you swim over here on to the other side of Annie Apple now and make your '**d...**' sound. Let's see whether together you have made the word **dad**!

Take your **dad** flashcard and explain that this *is* the word **dad**. Compare both Pictogram and plain sides to confirm that the letters are the same.

Have you made the same word? Yes? Yes! You have made the word **dad**!

Send your three children back to the left-hand side of the page to wait while you go over this new achievement. (Write **da, da-da** and **dad** on the board.) Let's see if you can make the word **dad** again.

Involve the others to help get the children in the right sequence. Remember, they can't see themselves, and they may not be very clear yet about thinking of the wall behind them as a big page. Having formed **dad** correctly, send the three back to the side of the room again.

da

da da

dad

Create 'add'

But **dad** is not the only word these three friends can make.

Have your **a** child come to the centre.

Now you two ducks hold hands and say '**d..**, **d..**, **d...**' together while you come over here.

In Letterland when you see two ducks together in a word they both make the same sound at exactly the same time so they sound more like *one* sound.

Have them form **add** and help the children to discover what word they have made. Compare it with **add** on the flashcards and **add** in **add an apple** learnt in STEP 2.

Picture Code Card Building

Leave the **a, d** and **d** picture code cards out where the children can handle them and sequence them to match your **add** and **dad** flashcards. (First use the Pictogram sides, then plain letter sides.)

First Dictionary

Award **d** stickers for learning all about Dippy Duck. Place on page 4 of the children's dictionary book. The children can already enter their first word – **dad**. They can also now enter **add** on their **a** page.

Code Sheet 3: dD

Follow the general instructions on page 149 and the points below.

Oral yellow ducks   different door colours down (direction)
          yellow daffodils   door handles/knobs   down (feathers)

Picture Coding   If felt pens are used, avoid smudging by having children colour yellow duck bodies and heads before overwriting the broken-line **d**'s. Congratulate all children who spot the second duck in **daffodil**!

First Spelling Picture: dad

A 'spelling picture' is a vivid way of emphasising both the phonic features of a word *and* its whole word meaning. You write the word in bold felt pen or paint. The children add the picture code to each letter and also draw the word's meaning above or all around it.

These 'spelling pictures' will speed up recognition of the vocabulary on the Code Sheets. Subsequently, use spelling pictures whenever you think a child will benefit from them. You can highlight *all* letters in a word or only one or two.

To read their own and each other's spelling pictures to the rest of a group or class, have a child point to the picture, say 'dad', or point to each apple, saying 'apple, apple,' etc. Finally he or she draws a finger across the word while reading it. (For more about spelling pictures see Step 7: **sS**, page 61).

Dippy Duck's dad.

First Quick Dash Routine

From now on start each Letterland session with a 'quick dash' through the picture code cards studied so far. Ask the following questions.

Teacher	Children
Who is this letter?	Clever Cat
What does she say in words?	**'c..'**
Who is this letter?	Annie Apple
What does she say in words?	**'a..'**
Who is this?	Dippy Duck
What does she say?	**'d..'**

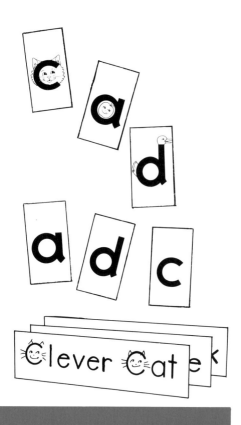

Now hold up the plain sides of each card and repeat the questions. Turn to the Pictogram side only to confirm answers.

Each new letter you teach should become part of your quick dash routine. Soon you can drop the questions. Just hold up the cards and challenge the children to give you the sounds only, in swift replies.

Also add your character name flashcards (Clever Cat, etc), to the routine dash. They will reinforce the capital letter shapes and whole word recognition at the same time.

A New Pace

So far you have introduced three Letterland characters in depth, taught picture coding, shown the children how to create words in 3-D, and been through reading exercises on flashcards and on the Code Sheets. You have strengthened their learning with music, interactive murals, the quick dash routine and spelling pictures.

In addition, make sure the children have practised writing the **c, a** and **d** shapes, not only on the Listen and Write Sheets, but in their own exercise books as well. Slightly older children will already be entering words in their first dictionaries, headed by the stickers they are earning for learning all about each letter.

You are now ready to introduce STEPS 4,5,6 and 7 (**h,m,t** and **s**) at an increased pace.

Wall Frieze aA – hH

Unfold your wall frieze to show up to **hH** or to **nN** if you like.

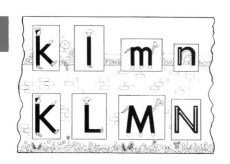

Hairy Hat Man

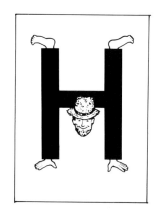

You will probably find that the Hairy Hat Man quietly becomes a hero in your Letterland teaching. Children like and admire him. With your encouragement, they might even model their behaviour on him, at times, by being ever so quiet because they know he hates noise!

(P) Flashcards

For this step you will need to prepare flashcards for these words.

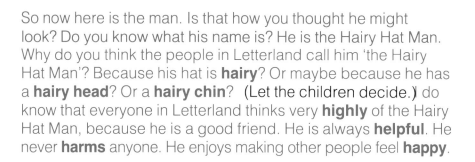

The Hat Man's Letter Shape

Now that the children are accustomed to expect a Pictogram design in each letter, change your approach. Present the letter **h** as a plain letter first and ask the children to suggest how the shape can be turned into a man. Ask "Where will his head be? His feet? What part of the letter becomes his back? His legs? Which way will he be going?" Then show the Pictogram side.

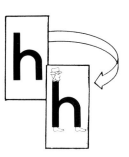

So now here is the man. Is that how you thought he might look? Do you know what his name is? He is the Hairy Hat Man. Why do you think the people in Letterland call him 'the Hairy Hat Man'? Because his hat is **hairy**? Or maybe because he has a **hairy head**? Or a **hairy chin**? (Let the children decide.) do know that everyone in Letterland thinks very **highly** of the Hairy Hat Man, because he is a good friend. He is always **helpful**. He never **harms** anyone. He enjoys making other people feel **happy**.

The Hat Man's Sound

There is a special thing you need to know about the Hairy Hat Man, and it is important. He **hates** noise. That is why he never speaks above a whisper. He can be quite **hard** to **hear**, so you'll have to be very quiet while I tell you what he says in words. He says '**hhh**'. Just like that, '**hhh**'. You whisper '**hhh**' too. '**Hhhh...hhhh...hhhh**'.

47

Have the children look closely at the card.

There is another funny thing about the Hairy Hat Man. Have you noticed? He has no shoes on, has he? I wonder why? (Discuss.) If you wanted to keep things as quiet as possible would you wear shoes? The Hairy Hat Man never wears shoes. You see he doesn't even want to hear the sound of his own footsteps because that makes it harder for him to hear himself whispering '**hhhh**'!

Write the Hat Man's Letter

Here is how the Hairy Hat Man likes you to write his letter.

| Air Trace | Finger Trace | Handwriting Verse | Listen and Write Sheet 4 | Involve Parents |

Be a Hat Man

You need a large room space for this.

Now you have met the Hairy Hat Man, can you tell me what he hates? (Noise!) So how does he speak? (In a whisper.) What does he say? (**Hhhh**.) Now I want you to listen for his '**hhhh**' sound as I tell you what to do next.

First, stand up and pretend you are the Hairy Hat Man. Let's hear you whispering his sound.

Now all move around the room (clockwise), whispering '**hhhh**'. Now stop.

Imagine a **hairy hat** on a table in front of you. Feel how **hhhairy** it is. Pick it up in your **hhhands**. Lift it **hhhigher**, and **hhhigher**, and put it on your **hhhead**. Make the Hairy Hat Man's sound again. '**Hhhh**.'

Now **hurry** along in the Reading Direction. Think of the wall near you as a great big page in a book and you are hurrying across the page. (Make sure the children understand this by demonstrating it.)

Stop now, and think of another way that the Hairy Hat Man might move. (Elicit 'hop'.) You **hop** whispering '**hhh, hhh, hhh**' with each hop.

Stop again. You are being much too noisy for Hairy Hat Man! No one can **hear** what you are whispering. Take off your shoes and then **hop** as quietly as you can while you whisper '**hhhh**'.

Find a partner and one of you lie down. Now the floor is your page and you are lying in a Hairy Hat Man shape. Remember to face the Reading Direction. Keep very still while your partner traces your shape. (Check each couple, giving each a turn at tracing.)

Sing about the Hat Man

Good, now we are all going to sit down again and sing the Hairy Hat Man Song (page 156).

Make sure the children whisper '**hhh...**' (a quick sigh, not 'huh') when they reach this point in the song.

Language Development with the Hat Man

Help the children to associate as many alliterative words as possible with the Hat Man character by discussing together the following.

- What his **house** might look like?
  Is it hat-shaped, like a haystack, humpy, high, hollow, hairy, huge, etc?
- What **hobbies** he might have?
  Hunting, playing hopscotch, hang gliding, being helpful, (holding hands to cross the street), making people happy?
- What he would like best to eat when he is **hungry**?
  Ham, honey, hamburgers, hot dogs, hazel nuts, hard-boiled eggs, etc?
- How he likes to travel on **holiday**?
  By helicopter, hovercraft, horseback, helium balloon, etc?

To follow up this language work later, paint pictures of him, including some of the objects arising from your discussion.

Capital H

You can always tell when the Hairy Hat Man is feeling particularly **happy**, because then he does his special trick. He does a **handstand** with his hat on!

Show capital **H** on the frieze and in the name of any children in the class (Helen, Henry, etc), and on the **Hairy Hat Man** flashcard.

Look! Here he is doing his handstand trick right here in (Helen's) name! Why do you think he is particularly happy at the beginning of her name? Names are important so the Hat Man always feels particularly happy when he is helping out with something important like starting a name.

Code Sheet 4: hH

Follow the general instructions and the points given below.

Oral hollow letters hates noise/hush hardly hear him
hold in your hand hurt/headache happier/-est

Picture Coding   Most children like adding hat, hair, feet, etc, and even the crudest drawing serves to animate this letter.

Revision   Re-read Code Sheets 1 to 3 (**cC, aA** and **dD**) to discover, listen to and code the **h**'s. Re-read Code Sheet 3 (**dD**) again, listening this time for Annie Apple's sound. Add apples inside all **a**'s.

3-D words: dad, had

Choose three children to revise the word **dad** in 3-D and create a new word: **had**. Afterwards leave the Picture Code Cards out so the children can reconstruct **add, dad** and **had** for themselves.

Hat Man Display

Paint a **huge** Hat Man and add labels for his hat, his head, his hands, etc. Let the children decide on the labels and draw pictures of objects beginning with his sound – hedgehogs, hamsters, hamburgers, etc.

Costume Box

If possible, make one or several hairy hats. They will come in handy both now and later when the children play-act the **sh** story (which proves how much the Hairy Hat Man hates noise!).

First Dictionary

Award **h** stickers for learning all about the Hairy Hat Man. Place on page 8. The word **had** can now be added.

Quick Dash Routine

Remember to start your next lesson with a quick dash, varying the order each day. Include relevant character names as well, and see if the children can match single letters to the character name flashcards.

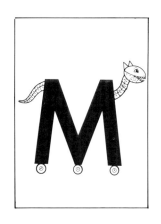

Munching Mike & his Mum

Munching Mike is a merry little monster. He is also mischievous, makes mistakes, and has a mighty appetite. But as monsters go he is a mild one, because he is still only little – just a mini-monster compared to his big, sharp-looking Mum (capital **M**).

You also have a second mini-monster card, Munching Maria. (Spot the differences – mouth and eyelashes!) Introduce her later when children want to spell not only **Mum** but **Mummy** and other words containing **mm**.

First develop Munching Mike's character with the children's help, by together finding many more words which start with his sound.

Introduce his Picture Code Card plain side first and let the children imagine how he might look before they see the Pictogram.

(P) Flashcards

Prepare these flashcards.

Munching Mike's Letter Shape

In Letterland there are some Mighty Mountains which look a bit like this. (Draw rough mountains similar to capital **M** on the board.)

These Mighty Mountains are the home of Munching Mike, the Metal Monster. On this card you can only see parts of this monster. His head and neck and tail are invisible, but can you tell me how many legs he has?

Yes, *three* legs. And instead of feet he has *three wheels*! Because he is a **metal** monster his legs, head, tail, wheels, and everything are made of metal.

Don't forget Munching Mike is a Letterland monster so which way will he be looking? Which way is the Reading Direction? (Elicit the correct answer looking at your wall sign.) Yes, that way. So at which end will Munching Mike's head be, and where will his tail be?

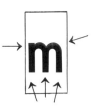

Let several children touch where the head, tail, and wheels will be on the plain **m**.

So now let's take a good look at Munching Mike the Metal Monster. Here he is! (Show Pictogram side.) Let's count his legs again. How do you think he moves? Yes, he rolls along on his three metal wheels!

Discuss what things are made of metal: window frames? table, chair, or trolley legs? pencil sharpener? magnets? etc.

Munching Mike's Sound

You can tell that Munching Mike loves his food because he keeps on saying '**Mmmm! Mmmm! Mmmm!**' with every mouthful. Can you be a munching monster and say '**Mmmm!**'?

Make sure everyone keeps their lips closed until they have finished the '**Mmmm**' sound. *Do not allow* a 'muh' sound.

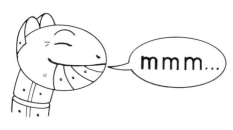

Munching Mike has an amazing appetite. He munches and munches but he only eats things that begin with his sound. So he munches **mints** by the mouthful. (Have children suggest other products beginning with **m**.)
He also munches **mats,**
        mushrooms and macaroni,
        maps and magazines,
        mops,
        metal magnets and machines.
And he has even been known to eat a whole **motorbike**! All these things just **melt** in his **metal mouth** and slip down his **metal** throat like **milk**.

Encourage the children to expand on what Mike might eat – the more far-fetched, the more fun and the more memorable – but exclude people, e.g. **men** or **mums**, because Munching Mike thinks they taste 'monstrous'!

Write Munching Mike's Letter

Air Trace

Finger Trace

Handwriting Verse

Listen and Write

Involve Parents

Wall Frieze: a-r and A-R

By now you can mount your alphabet frieze as far as **rR** so that the children will see Munching Mike and his Mum, plus some of the characters they will soon meet. Tell the children who the new characters are, if asked.

Capital M

Do you remember how Clever Cat made herself look bigger? (Let the children *tell* you and *show* you by breathing in deeply). Well, Munching Mike would like to make himself bigger too. But he is not quite old enough to do it properly yet! So for the time being Munching Mike just leaves the job of starting important words to his Mum. Since Munching Mike's Mum is much bigger, she munches much more than her son and says '**MMM**' even louder as she munches.

Show the **Munching Mike** flashcard..

This is Munching Mike's name. See his Mum looking big and sharp, *twice*, to start the two words of his name for him? Names are important words. Now who do we have right here in our classroom whose names begin with Munching Mike's Mum?

Make name paintings and display them. Identify names that have Munching Mike and Munching Maria inside them as well, e.g. Emma, and compare his size with his Mum's size according to position and function.

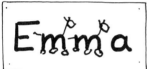

Play-Act, Sing about the Monster

See page 156 for Munching Mike's song. Mime him and his Mum (using either one or three children to make a monster).

3-D word: ham

Now, Munching Mike is going to help us discover the Hairy Hat Man's favourite food.

Choose three children, one to be the Hat Man, another to be Annie Apple, and another to be Munching Mike.

Sequence two children as **h a**. Adapt the blending verse on page 42 used for 'da..'. Then call your **m** child over to say '**mmm**'. Help the children to discover that the sounds, put together equal the word **ham**.

Let the rest of the class compare the flashcard **ham** with the children's sequence. Confirm that **ham** *is* the Hat Man's favourite food – ham with honey on it, to be exact!

Munching Mike at Marlfield Farm
First School, Redditch, Worcs.

53

Strengthen the Blend Strategy

Use the Picture Code Cards to develop the art of blending:

- Get ready to whisper the Hat Man's '**hhh...**' sound, but don't say it yet.
- Get ready to make Annie Apple's '**ă...**' sound.
- Now let both sounds burst out of your mouth together: '**ha...!**'
- Now add Munching Mike's '**mmm...**' sound and the word is...? **Ham**! (Bring your **m** card over to complete the word.)

This 'store up and release' method is simply another way of stressing the blending verse 'Don't make my sound all alone' on page 42. Leave the **h, a** and **m** cards on a table where the children can turn them over to combine either picture or plain sides to make **ham** again themselves.

Letterland Characters Everywhere!

By now the children are likely to want to picture code all the letters in all their names. Picture code as many names as you can and if the children ask about letters you have not covered yet, tell them briefly about the characters. There is no harm in looking ahead. Remember to box letters that make atypical sounds, and write silent letters in dots.

Code Sheet 5: mM

Follow the general instructions and the points below.

Oral metal mouth munch   mid-day meal   magnets
melt metal   chew/crunch   more and more magnetic

Picture Coding   Pencil will serve for drawing a metal head, tail and wheels. Use light blue or mauve if available. Help children to deduce what to draw in the empty box over the word **mat**.

Revision   Re-read Code Sheets 1 to 4 (**c, a, d** and **h**). Discover, listen to and code **m** on sheets 2 to 4. Revise **d** on Sheet 5 (**m**) by overwriting them in thick orange.

First Dictionary

Award **m** stickers for learning all about Munching Mike. The word **mat** can be added after the next STEP.

Quick Dash: a,c,d,h,m

Remember to begin each Letterland session with this routine. Use the five Picture Code Cards to revise sounds. Use the character name flashcards to reinforce capital letter recognition and rapid whole word recognition.

Ticking Tess

Communication in Letterland is a little more simple than in everyday life – Ticking Tess and Ticking Tom team up to do it *all* with tiny ticks. Two Picture Code Cards are provided for **t** because many words are spelt with **tt**. The function of double letters is treated fully in the Main Pack. Tess is introduced first to congrue with current editions of the Letterland ABC where she appears, instead of Tom, to ensure a better ethnic and gender balance. Use Tess or Tom to match your edition.

(P) Flashcards

Have ready these flashcards.

 *

Ticking Tess's Shape and Sound

Now meet Ticking Tess who works in the Letterland Teletouch Tower. She is a tall straight letter and she loves to work in her tall straight tower, surrounded by telephones, tape recorders and televisions sets.

Ticking Tess

When people want to get in touch with each other in Letterland they just tell Ticking Tess to start ticking. In no time at all she sends messages in all directions! How does she do it? Just by talking into her machines in tiny, tiny ticks!

I am going to whisper the tiny ticking sound that Ticking Tess makes. It's like this: **t..,t..,t..,t..,t...** Can *you* whisper Ticking Tess's sound? Let me hear you.

Now listen again. I **t**ick with the **t**ip of my **t**ongue, **t..,t..,t...** Can you say that with me?

Hold up your **telephone** flashcard and have everyone repeat the word several times so that they really hear the **t** sound at the beginning.

(*You may also find it useful to make a Ticking Tom flashcard.)

Write Ticking Tess's Letter

Finger Trace

Handwriting Verse

Listen and Write Sheet

Involve Parents

Capital T

Ticking Tess can make herself even taller when she takes a deep breath – so tall that her head disappears in the clouds! Then all you can see of her is her tall, straight body, her arms and maybe, if you are lucky, a telephone in her hand.

Play-Act, Sing about Ticking Tess

Sing Ticking Tess's song (see page 157) and act out her shape and sound. The children stretch out their arms, softly tick, and turn on their tip toes. Avoid 'tuh' sounds by whispering.

3-D Words: hat, cat, mat

Appoint four children to be **h, a, t** and **c**.

Today the Hairy Hat Man and Annie Apple feel like making a word. So they stand together and say ...? (**hă...**) Right! But that isn't a word is it? So they call Ticking Tess to come over and add her sound. You call her. Here she comes ticking along, getting ready to tick next to them. Let's see if they have made a word now. **Ha..t, ha..t, hat**. Yes, **hat** is a word!

Go over this again helping the children discover: **ha..t**. It helps to have a real hat available to convey meaning – the real thing and the *word* for it. Next, organise the children to make **cat**.

Now the Hairy Hat Man sees Clever Cat. He knows she *loves* being in words so he says, 'Here, Clever Cat. You can have my place.' He hops off in the Reading Direction while in comes Clever Cat. So now what word have these three friends made together?

Go on to discover **at** and make **mat**. Back up with the Picture Code Cards as needed.

Code Sheet 6: tT

Follow the general instructions and the points below.

Oral tall tower   tan (or turquoise) tie   tangerine/fruit/colour
     tree tops   twins, two of a kind   talk to over distance

Picture Coding Children code head, feet, earphones and telephone in tan, turquoise, tangerine (orange) or teal (green). Turn her toes in the Reading Direction.

Revision Re-read Code Sheets 1-5: **c,a,d,h** and **m**. Discover Ticking Tess's letter on each one and code it. (There are none on Sheet 3 but scanning for a letter is a useful skill to exercise in its own right.)

First Dictionary

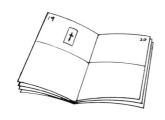

Award a **t** sticker to each child for learning all about Ticking Tess. Place on page 19 of their exercise books.

More Spelling Pictures: hat, cat

Write or paint the words **hat** and **cat**. Distribute enough copies for two different groups of children to picture code *and* illustrate their meanings.

When they have finished, have some children in the **hat** group take turns pointing at each of their hats saying '**hat, hat, ...**' and then '**hat**' again as they slide their finger across the words. Help them to end with their finger at the **t** as they pronounce this sound at the end.

Do a similar routine with the **cat** spelling pictures and the earlier ones of **mat**, giving the children practice with each others' words.

Follow up by letting the children construct **hat, cat** and **mat** in Picture Code Cards, using Pictogram sides first, then plain sides. If they make non-words, let them try to pronounce them to you, and treat them as fun.

Quick Dash

Start your next Letterland lesson with a dash of the letters and character name flashcards learnt so far.

c	**Clever Cat**	h	**Hairy Hat Man**
a	**Annie Apple**	m	**Munching Mike**
d	**Dippy Duck**	t	**Ticking Tess**

Let the children handle, discuss and identify the single word flashcards: **cat, apple, duck, dad, hat** and **ham**.

Use any of the Action Sentences that are suitable, listed on the Scope and Sequence Chart.

Sammy Snake

If, like **s**, every letter of the alphabet were as instantly evocative of a creature that actually makes that letter's sound, there would have been no need for Letterland! Make the most of Sammy Snake. He will help you not only to teach shape and sound but also to explain the function of **s** as a plural signal. Sammy and his sister Sally Snake, together on a further Picture Code Card will help you to teach **ss**.

Ⓟ Flashcards

| snake | snakes | Sammy Snake | Sally Snake |

Sammy's Shape

Sammy Snake is a **sweet** little **smiling** snake, not a **scary** snake at all. He is happy as long as you **stroke** him properly – **start** at the top of his head and **smooth** down his **scales** to his tail and he will **smile** all day long.

Have a child kneel in a snake-like **s** position and let some other children stroke Sammy the way he likes it. Emphasise *from the top of his head* – and the 'snake' can smile and hiss his thanks.

ssss...

Sammy Snake's Sound

Sammy Snakes spends most of his time in words hissing away like this, '**sss,sss,sss**'. He hisses as he **slips** and **slides** and **slithers** along in the Reading Direction. If you lisssten carefully you will hear him hisssing in lotsss and lotsss of words. Have the children pronounce a few suitable words slowly, exaggerating the **s** sound so that they really feel the '**sss**' sound escaping from between their teeth. See if they can say: '**S**ammy **S**nake like**s** to **s**it be**s**ide the **s**ea.'

Sssammy Sssnake likesss to sssit by the sssea.

sss

Write Sammy Snake's Letter

Air
Trace

Finger
Trace

Handwriting
Verse

Listen and
Write Sheet

Involve
Parents

Capital S

Sammy Snake takes a deep breath and gets bigger. He says "Now I'm a super-size snake"!

Show on your **Sammy Snake** flashcard how much bigger Sammy has made himself than all the other letters in his name.

Wall Frieze: aA – vV

Unfold your wall frieze to show up to **vV**, leaving **w – z** and **W – Z** folded out of sight. Compare 'small' Sammy with 'super-size' Sammy.

Play-
Act

Sing
Song

3-D Words

Make **sad, sam, sat** and **mat** by substituting children. Let them discover each time what new word they have made. Ensure good initial blends by prolonging the '**sss**' and '**mmm**' sounds: **ssssa..** and **mmmma..** with NO PAUSE before **ǎ.**

For other good words to make in 3-D, see your Scope and Sequence Chart.

Code Sheet 7: sS

Oral slither sad/sorry   sunny smile   Sammy's size
slide   cross/angry sunny sky/sea sister Sally's size (same)

Picture Coding   Overwrite broken-line **s**'s. Add head, tail. Add missing item: the sun's smile.

Revision   Re-read Sheets **c,a,d,h,m** and **t** (1 – 6). Discover, listen, code or just overwrite **s**'s in thick yellow or green. Also code **h** and **H** on Sheet 7.

First Dictionary

Award **s** stickers. Place on page 19. The words **sad, Sam** (or **sam**), and **sat** can now be entered. Also **mat** on the **m** page.

59

Sounding like Z (Sleepy Sammy)

You have taught the voiceless hissing sound, but a close analysis of the sound of **s** in common words shows that six out of ten contain not a hissing sound but **s** sounding exactly like **z** (for example, in **is, his, has, was, comes, goes, lives, plays, these, boys, girls, cars,** etc). Therefore, present Sammy as having two kinds of hiss – his 'wide awake hiss' (**sss**), and his 'sleepy hiss' (**zzz**). The STEP for **z** comes at the end of this manual not only because **z** ends the alphabet, but also to make sure that children link both '**sss**' and '**zzz**' to **s** first.

One reason everyone likes Sammy Snake is because he works hard. He *has* to work hard because *so many* words need his hissing sound. He has to dash about and be in so many places that he doesn't have time to sleep all night, so instead he has lots of *very quick* snoozes in the daytime, just for a few seconds each time. In some words you can hear him snoozing because his hisses don't sound like this, '**sss**', anymore. Instead, they sound like this: '**zzzz**'.

You listen for his snoozing sound while I speak these words slowly: **boys, girls, eyes, hands, ears.** And now here is a word with *two* quick snoozes: **noses.** Did you hear Sammy's two snoozes?

Have the children mime Sammy hissing, then snoozing, and then swiftly waking up again: **sss, zzz, sss**!

Next, set the children to wondering how often Sammy Snake manages a quick snooze in words. Devote wall space to two lists with paintings of Sammy Snake at the top of each – one wide awake and one snoozing – and let the children put words in the correct column.

It should emerge that Sammy is prone to a snooze beside certain letters (the voiced ones) and never beside certain other ones (the whispered or unvoiced letters).

Sammy at the End (Plurals)

Re-use the children's **cat** and **hat** spelling pictures to draw attention to the ends of words and then to Sammy Snake's function in forming the appropriate plurals. Do this as follows.

Have the children point to each *picture* of a hat, saying 'hat, hat, hat'. Then they point to the *word* **hat** and slide their finger across the word as they read (as described before).

Next, hold up the Sammy Snake card and help them to hear Sammy's hiss at the end – '**hatsss**' meaning more than one hat (*several* hats, as in the picture).

The children can make their own separate Sammy Snake cards and add them to, and remove them from, the picture.
Use the same routine to help them read each other's **cat** pictures.
Encourage the children to show you and tell you in their own words what Sammy is doing (adding his hiss to change the meaning of the word).

Revise Plurals on Flashcards

Cat, cats, hat, hats, duck, ducks, apple, apples.

Ask the children to pick out the words in which Sammy Snake hisses, and the *one* in which he has a quick snooze (**apples**).

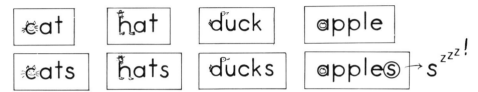

Double Letters: Sammy Snake and his Sister Sally

No less than 15 letters of the alphabet are frequently doubled, generally because the doubling signals a new meaning (e.g. **of, off**) or serves a special function (e.g. **hop, hopping**). The formal explanation for these doubled letters is, as usual, too technical to be of interest to children. The Letterland explanations are quite simple and of two kinds – one for shared sounds (covered in the Starter Pack), another for silent letters (covered in the Main Pack).

As in STEP 3 with **dd** in the word **add**, explain **ss** as a 'shared sound'. Sammy and his sister Sally *both* hiss at exactly the same time in some words because the word needs them both, e.g. **his** but **hiss.**

Sammy Snake has a sister called Sally Snake who loves hissing just as much as he does, and you will often see them hissing *together*.

Ask the children to go 'snake spotting', i.e. looking for words where Sammy and Sally occur side by side. They can make a collection of words, cutting them from magazines and newspaper headlines, etc. (Also ask the children if they can find any words in which Sammy and Sally have a quick snooze *together*.)

Follow up. Make snakes with many different skins: spotted, striped, with stars, spangles or scale patterns – even silver-skinned snakes. (These can all be Sammy and Sally when they shed skins!) Then play counting games using the action sentences: **add Sammy Snake** and **add Sally Snake**.

3-D Words: his, hiss

See your Scope and Sequence Chart for more 3-D Words to make.

Now or Later: sh

If, in your judgement, the children are ready for the **sh** story, remind them that the Hairy Hat Man hates noise, so when they see Sammy Snake beside the Hairy Hat Man in a word, the new sound is '**sh**!'

When Sammy Snake comes slithering and sliding up behind the Hairy Hat Man in a word, do you think the Hat Man is going to put up with all that noise? (No!) So what does he do? He turns back and says '**sh**!' to hush Sammy up.

So whenever you see Sammy and the Hat Man side by side in a word, don't expect their usual '**sss**' and '**hhh**' sounds. Expect one big '**sh**!' sound instead.

Divide the children into snakes and Hat Men. Their play-acting of this story will help to reinforce it in their minds. Also have them sing the **sh** song on Letterland Audio Tape No. 1. The words can be found in the accompanying songbook.

Code Sheet 32: sh

Follow the general instructions and the points below.

Oral he/she   dish/wish/fish   fish shop   should (be hot/wet) cold, shiver swish/swoosh ship (she) should think so!

Picture Code Listen, code **sh** in **she** and **dish**. Write **yes, no** and **she, he** where needed.

Revision Code all vowels on this sheet, either now or at a later date according to the children's needs. If they are already proficient in handling the short and long vowels, omit any further coding of vowels until you introduce the stories explaining the new vowel sounds (e.g. **ai, oa, ou, oo,** etc in the Main Pack).

Fawbert and Barnard Primary, Old Harlow, Essex.

Revision of Steps 1 – 7

Quick Dash

Start your revision with a dash of the letters **c,a,d,h,m,t,s,ss** and the appropriate character names. Include **sh** if taught.

Ear-First Game: dD, hH, aA, cC, mM

This game practises auditory discrimination of initial sounds. Ask each child to draw **hH** and **dD** on both sides of two separate cards, and add picture codes on one side only. If necessary, help them by writing the letters for them but let them do the picture coding.

Ask the children to hold up the correct card (**dD** or **hH**) for the sound they hear at the beginning of each of the following:

1. **dreary day**
2. **heavy hammer**
3. **dozing donkey**
4. **hillside house**
5. **dark door**
6. **hole**
7. **dusty desk**
8. **dessert**
9. **diving**
10. **hunting**
11. **hopping**
12. **digging**
13. **hitting**
14. **dancing**
15. **day dreaming**
16. **hippopotamus**

On a subsequent day the children make and use **cC** and **aA** cards to hold up when they hear the initial sound. The following day do the same with **dD** and **cC**.

cC/aA
1. **cold cabbage**
2. **appetising apple**
3. **crazy costume**
4. **angry alligator**
5. **canoe**
6. **ant**
7. **camera**
8. **coffee-coloured curtain**
9. **arrow**
10. **candle**
11. **ankle**
12. **caravan**

dD/cC
1. **dancing daisies**
2. **clean cups**
3. **damp dog**
4. **deep ditch**
5. **cosy cushions**
6. **coughing cowboy**
7. **copy cats**
8. **danger**
9. **coconut cream**
10. **delicious dinner**
11. **dandelion**
12. **colourful caterpillar**

On subsequent days do combinations of **mM/dD** and **mM/hH**.

1. **marshamallows**
2. **dry doughnuts**
3. **merry music**
4. **mouldy mushrooms**
5. **dizzy dancers**
6. **magazines**
7. **muffins**
8. **ding dong**
9. **my mother**
10. **dandelions**
11. **mixed mints**
12. **misty mountains**

1. **moonlight**
2. **haystack**
3. **medicine**
4. **head over heels**
5. **helicopter**
6. **meadow**
7. **hollow handle**
8. **headache**
9. **magic mark**
10. **milestone**
11. **heated house**
12. **more meat**

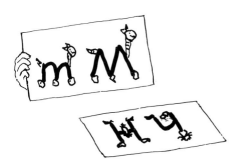

Watch out for any children making many mistakes. Arrange to play the game with them on a one-to-one basis later. This may help you to identify children with hearing loss or poor auditory perception.

The Hat Man's Hat Rack

Prepare flashcards for **add a hat, add 2 hats** and **add 3 hats**.

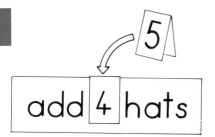

Draw a hat rack and have the children paint detachable hats to stick on it, depending on which card you hold up. You can also overlay other numbers – 4, 5, 6, etc – if you wish.

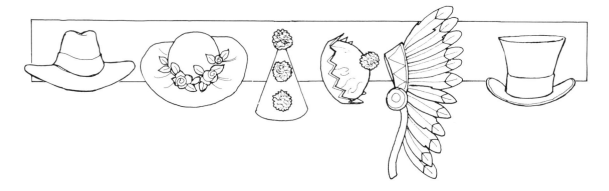

How Many Hats?

Hand out your flashcards for **cat, hat, hats, apple** and **duck,** and help the children to construct the following:

1 cat hat
1 apple hat
2 duck hats
2 cat hats
3 apple hats
4 duck hats

Remind the children how Sammy's hiss at the end of the word **hats** tells us that we have more than one. Use the phrase *ssseveral of something* where appropriate.

Frieze Games

Take both small and capital letter or just capital letter sections of the wall frieze into a large room. Mount **aA – vV** leaving **wW – zZ** still folded out of sight. Hand out the seven Picture Code Cards learnt so far to seven children. Have others take turns calling out a character name. The child holding that card must run to the frieze and match either the small to small or small to capital letter. Repeat using sounds instead of character names. As the number of letters grow, develop races between two children to different parts of the full **A–Z** frieze. (See page 143.)

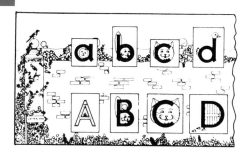

Spelling Pictures

Headbands

Make more headbands for the costume box. See page 160 for illustrations of simple ones to make.

Shopping Game: Revising t,d,s

Before you move on to the next STEP, play the Shopping Game to help develop listening skills and to give practice in answering in complete sentences.

One day Ticking Tom went shopping, but he only bought things beginning with his '**t...**' sound.

Have the children answer *'Yes!'* and repeat your sentence with **t** items in it, or *'No!'* and stay silent.

Teacher	Ticking Tom bought **ten tangerines** and took them home to his tower. Ten tangerines?
Children	Yes! Ticking Tom bought ten tangerines and took them home to his tower.
Teacher	Ticking Tom bought a **tape-recorder** and took it home to his tower. Tape-recorder?

65

| *Children* | Yes! (They repeat full sentence.) |
| *Teacher* | Ticking Tom bought a **tube of toothpaste** and took it home to his tower. Tube of toothpaste? |

Children	Yes! (They repeat full sentence.)
Teacher	Ticking Tom bought a **dancing doll** and took it home to his tower. Dancing doll?
Children	No! (They shake their heads in silence.)

Other items you can use include **daffodils, strong suitcase, tan typewriter, television table, spiced sausages, toy train, drum and drumsticks, soft slippers, tin telescope**, etc.

The children can follow this up by drawing a picture of Ticking Tom with some of the things he has bought.

3-D Copying

The children have now been presented with seven letter shapes and grouped these to make words. Now show them how to 'keep their own words' by writing them down on paper.

Develop the idea of writing as a means of remembering, e.g. mother's shopping list, cake recipe, names of people in a telephone book etc.

Use 3-D copying first. The children simply 'write down their friends', sequenced to make **hat, mat** and then **ham.**.

Then follow 3-D copying by slow-speak spelling. Your aim is to slow down words which the child wants to spell so that he can begin to spell by ear.

Slow-Speak Spelling

Introduce 'slow-speak' as your new way of speaking, from time to time. (See page 20.)

I think the Hairy Hat Man really likes his hairy *hhha...t*, don't you?
Do you think he would *mmminnnd* if Clever Cat *sssa...t* on it?
What if she *sssa...t innn* it?

Have the children slow-speak **hat, mind, in,** etc, too.
Having used some slow-speak in living speech, you are ready to have the children write down some slow-speak words as you say them, e.g. **sat, hat,** and soon **in, on** etc.

Review the correct handwriting strokes on the board, with white chalk. Then see if the children can write the word **mat** from your dictation. (Do this slowly – *mmmmaaaa...t*.) Use the blackboard to help *only* if necessary. Review this by using the Picture Code Cards to show the blending.

Moving from speech to paper is an important skill to start early. Mix this type of writing session with more Picture Code Card word building where there are numerous opportunities to discuss the sounds as the children form the words.

Some words are easier to slow-speak than others without having to pause between ANY of the sounds, causing distortion. Useful examples are highlighted in your Scope and Sequence Chart No.1. Use them regularly with each letter.

Chart No. 1

Action Sentences	3-D Words	Slow-Speak	Code Sheet Words
	(Underlining indicates useful slow-speak words)		*(excluding Flashcard Words)*
add a cat			a, add, caterpillar
add an apple add 2 apples			an, Applestand, ant, sad, happy
add Ticking Tom	at, mat, hat, cat		can, tick, and, has, twin, Tess
add Sammy Snake	Sam, sat, sad, had has, hat, hats, cats		cross, Sam, in the, sand His, sister, Sally
Hiss at (any character name). Hiss at his hat.	it, is, his, hiss, miss, him, hat, hit, hid, did		This, Fill, with, pen, in it, drip, drop
Act like Sammy Snake. Act like (any character name).	I am, I can kind/find		I am, I like, ice, kind, nice

Sentence Progression: Chart No. 2

Go over the sentences on Scope and Sequence Chart No. 2, Steps 1 – 7 (**c – s**), for both oral and silent reading practice. Set them out as described on the Chart. (For overhead projection, use permanent black for the words. Use non-permanent colours to add, then wipe off, any picture coding which you find the children still need.)

You will find no special logo for sentence progression in the text to remind you to take advantage of this Chart. It is assumed that you will use its sentence progression within every Step, especially in those teaching situations where no structured reading scheme is in operation.

Consonant Capers

The Consonant Capers verses do more than practise blends. They can help non-readers to start reading (page 159), widen slow readers' vocabulary and develop better eye movements as they read in time to the music. Bold lettering ensures that they notice each blend again and again.

Now that you have completed Steps 1–7 you may like to introduce the **sc, sm** and **st** capers.

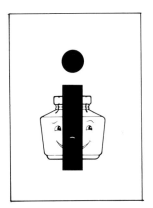

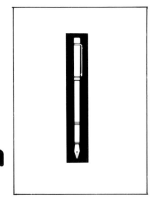

Impy Ink, the Ink Pen & Mr I

Three words beginning with **i** are among the 12 most-used words in the English language: **in, is** and **it**. **Is** and **it** are taught in this STEP. (See STEP 9 for **in**.)

First it may be useful to bring to school a real ink pen and a real bottle of ink. The fact that ink is not sold everywhere these days should not deter you. It is still available in many colours in art shops. Ink also remains an essential ingredient in printing. So children still need to know what ink is, even if they only see it these days flowing from the tips of their felt pens. Then go on to present a very special bottle of ink called 'Impy Ink', a friendly and sometimes mischievous little fellow who plays an important part in everyone's life in Letterland.

In this STEP you will also be referring casually to the Vowel Man 'Mr I'. Some attention to 'long i' is essential as **I** is another of the 12 most-used English words. Your pack of Picture Code Cards includes the word **I** so that you can work with such phrases as '**I am, I can,**' etc.

(P) Mural and Flashcards

You may like to create an 'ink and ice cream' mural to start this STEP. It should show Mr I with a vendor's cart which has two sections – one for **ink** and one for **ice cream.**

Make and hand out large enough **i**'s for the children to picture code with ink bottles. They add these to the foreground of the mural by slipping them into Mr I's Ink Bin. (You can make one out of transparent plastic).

You will also need an ice cream cone, simply made out of paper, to help you introduce Mr I.

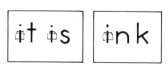

ink bin

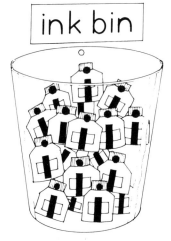

68

Introducing Impy Ink

In Letterland ink is important because *every* child in *every* school in Letterland writes with an *ink pen*. You see, there are no pencils in Letterland, and no felt pens. You *can* buy crayons, but they are too thick to write with. So everyone who wants to write anything down needs an ink pen and some ink to put in it.

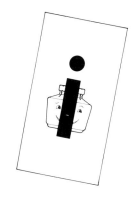

Luckily in Letterland there is a nice man called Mr I who sells lots of ink, and ink pens. He sells ink in many different colours – he sells red ink, blue ink, green ink, pink ink and lots of other colours too, all in little ink bottles.

There are *some* ink bottles though, which Mr I will not sell. They are his very special *talking* ink bottles. Who ever heard of an ink bottle that could talk? **Im**possible you might think, but not in Letterland. Let me tell you about one of them, Impy Ink! (Hold up Pictogram card.) Does he look as though he is about to wink? He has an impish face, and he does have a habit of winking every few minutes. Can any of you wink like Impy Ink? (Let the children try.)

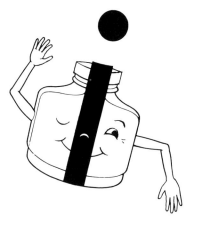

Impy Ink's Shape

Can you think why people call this talking ink bottle '**Impy Ink**'? It might just be because he likes to play tricks. Shall I tell you Impy Ink's favourite trick? He spills ink! Just a spot, mind you. But every time you see him in a word you will see a little spot of ink over his head. Why do you think he does it?

Discuss possible reasons. Lead the children to decide that maybe this is Impy Ink's tricky little way of helping children to recognise him quickly in words, because his letter is so thin and little without a dot above it. Conclude that Impy Ink is a good friend to all children learning to read.

Impy Ink's Sound

Impy Ink has lots of talking friends. We don't know all their names but one is called 'Isabel Ink' and another is 'Ingrid Ink'. What sound do you think Impy Ink and his friends make in words?

Help the children to isolate the ĭ sound at the start of his name and then chorus it.

Write Impy Ink's Letter

Air
Trace

Finger
Trace

Handwriting
Verse

Listen and
Write Sheet

Involve
Parents

Important Little Words: it, is

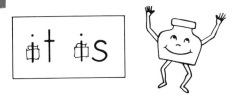

You will often hear Impy Ink making his little 'ĭ' sound right at the beginning of these two little words: **it is.** (Hold up your flashcard.)

Sound out the words together. Then draw an animated ink bottle on the board and put your **it is** flashcard beside it. Elicit 'It is Impy Ink'.

Yes, it is Impy Ink. Can you hear Impy's little 'ĭ' sound in **it**? Can you hear it again in **is**? And in Impy's own name: Impy Ink? (Do not show the **Impy Ink** flashcard yet.)

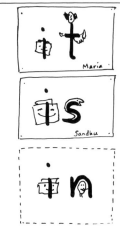

Discuss how often we need these little words to say, for example, the following.

It is raining	**It is silly**	**It is an insect**
It is time to play	**It is important**	**It is an ink pen**
It is late	**It is interesting**	**It is an ink bottle**

Decide together that **it is important** to be able to read little words which we use very often.

Let every child make their own spelling pictures of **it** and **is**. This time they will be able to picture code only the letters.

Explain that some words help us to name things which we can draw. But other words like these two are different. They help us to talk *about* hundreds of things we cannot picture.

Display **it** and **is** under the heading 'Important Words', picture coded by two children.

3-D Words: it, is

More words are listed on your Scope and Sequence Chart.

Add a character name flashcard to make little sentences, and listen together to the ĭ sounds in all three names.

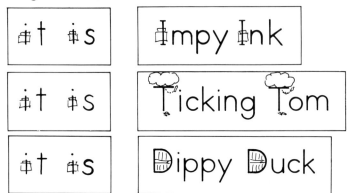

Also make living sentences by placing **it is** beside a child whose name contains Impy Ink's sound, e.g. Philip, Linda.

70

Capital I: Short Sound

Remember how some Letterland people and animals tell us that they are starting an important word by taking a deep breath and getting bigger? Well, when Impy Ink takes a deep breath his letter gets so tall and thin that you can't see his ink spot anymore. His letter looks like an ink pen instead of a little line with a dot.

If you are lucky you may see an ink pen in it (point to the frieze) or...you may see Impy Ink himself, looking just a little bigger and ever so important – just like on this sign which says 'Important Words'. (Coding on other letters is optional.)

Code Sheet 8: ĭ, Ĭ

Oral

ink	imp/impish	dip/drip	in-vis-ible
ink pen	insects	fill/spill	invisible ink trick

Picture Coding Code both small **i** and capital **I** with a light blue ink bottle to indicate 'short i'. (While the ink *pen* Pictogram on the frieze stresses the capital letter shape, it cannot be drawn inside handwritten **I**'s.) Overwrite **i**'s and add ink bottles in blue. As always, have children confirm the sound before coding it.

Revision Re-read Code Sheets **c,a,d,h,m,t** and **s** (1 – 7). Discover, listen and code ink bottles (little blue squares will do) through each letter *only if* it looks and sounds like Impy Ink. (All but one will. Keen listeners might discover Mr I saying 'I' in **Mike**.

First Dictionary

Award **i** stickers for learning all about Impy Ink. Place on page 9. Leave room for each child to add a stick man. Also divide the page in two, so 'ink words' can be added on the left and 'Mr I words' on the right. (There will be relatively few entries on this page.) Add **it** and **is** now. Add the word **I** at the end of this STEP.

Capital I

Since long **I** in the *word* **I** will very soon be needed for your language experience work (writing under the children's pictures), you may wish to give priority now to long **I**.

By introducing Mr I as selling *two* products, ink and ice cream, you can immediately use the essential word **I** and follow on with another high-usage word – **like** – without contradicting your short **i** teaching.

Mr I is everyone's friend because he supplies n**i**ce tasty **i**ce cream in Letterland. Any child can play-act being Mr I by handing out lots of imaginary ice creams. (Others can play at receiving and licking them.)

Using your paper ice cream cone, talk about Mr I roughly as follows.

Do you like ice cream? Well then, if you went to Letterland who is the first person you might like to meet?

Elicit Mr I and show his capital letter Picture Code Card.

Yes! Mr I, the Ice Cream Man! Everyone says that his ice cream tastes very, very nice. He has all *kinds* of tasty ice creams for you to buy. Mr I is a Vowel Man just like...who else do we know who is a Vowel man?(Elicit Mr A, the Apron Man from Asia.) So now we have met *two* Vowel Men, Mr A and Mr I.

Play-act, sing about Impy Ink and Mr I

Hold up your ink card until the last line. Then hold up the capital **I** card. (Choose the right moment to introduce your small **i** card showing Mr I there too. The cards themselves will do more than anything you can say, explaining visually that Impy Ink and Mr I share both the **i** and **I** shapes.)

Hold up your flashcard for **Mr I** next to the flashcard for **I am**. Give your paper cone to a child to hold high in his or her right hand while reading out sentences. Other children can take their turn while you point to each word as they say it. Substitute other name flashcards to make:

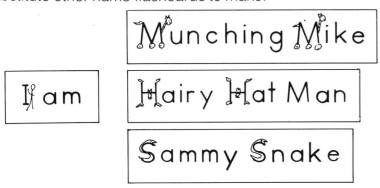

I am	Munching Mike
	Hairy Hat Man
	Sammy Snake

Have different children hold up the cards for the others to read in chorus. Then make the appropriate character's sound each time.

Follow on with your **I like** flashcard and use the name cards again:

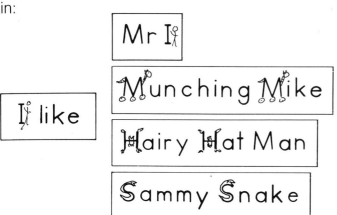

	Mr I
I like	Munching Mike
	Hairy Hat Man
	Sammy Snake

72

Other possibilities, using the flashcards you have made, are:

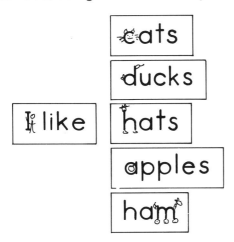

You could also hold up the **I like** flashcard next to the children's name paintings on the wall.

Code Sheet 29: Mr I

Now or Later

Oral Mr I   Mr I likes   ice cream   nice
      I (self)   I like   right kind   polite

Picture Coding Confirm in each word, ink bottle? Or Mr I himself? (Only one ink bottle is needed to code a short **i** – in the word **in**.) Overwrite and complete the stick men in blue.

Revision Later re-read Code Sheets 9 – 16. Discover, listen to and picture code Mr I in all capital **I**'s.

Follow Up

Action Sentences   3-D Word Making   3-D Word Copying   Slow-Speak   Spelling Pictures   Quick Dash

See your Scope and Sequence Chart for words to use in any or all of these routines.

STEP 9
Naughty Nick & his Nails

Naughty Nick is typical of every young boy who means well but cannot help being naughty every so often. By introducing him now, you can focus on the word **no** well in advance of the word **on**, and so help to avoid typical early confusions between **on** and **no**.

You also prepare the way for yes/no responses (starting on Code Sheet 10: **yY**) designed to ensure that the children will read for meaning. Your Naughty Nicola Picture Code Card is interchangeable with the Naughty Nick one. (Her vital role in predicting when to spell words with **nn** is explained fully in the Main Pack.)

Ⓟ Flashcards

| Naughty Nick | no | can | man | in |

Naughty Nick and his Nickname

There is a naughty boy who lives in Letterland. His name is Naughty Nick. (Show Pictogram side of card. Exaggerate **n**'s.) **N**aughty **N**ick is a **nice** boy, really, but unfortunately he does like to be **naughty** quite often. He can also be very **nosy**, which is a **nuisance**. And he is **noisy**. He loves hammering **nails** which grown-ups especially find very a**nn**oying. (Point to the nail in the **n**.)

See how he always has at least one **nail** with him? Another annoying habit of Nick's is saying '**No**!' He likes saying '**No**' even when he knows he should be saying 'Yes'.

When his mother says it's bedtime, Naughty Nick always says '**No**! **NNN**ot yet!' Sometimes he shouts so loudly he disturbs all the **neighbours**.

Once Naughty Nick did something so naughty with some nails that people **nicknamed** him '**Naughty Nick Nails**'. And that has been his **nickname** ever since!

Allow discussion. Leave the children to wonder what very naughty thing Naughty Nick did to earn his nickname. Meanwhile the topic of naughtiness is likely to elicit a good deal of language from children, based on their own experience!

Find a suitable time to use the crooked sign on the Frieze, left hand pillar, as one small piece of proof of Naughty Nick's naughtiness. That sign used to be **nailed** in straight but... has anyone **noticed** how it looks **now**? Guess who... etc.

Naughty Nick's Letter Shape and Sound

Naughty Nick's letter starts with a straight line, just like a nail. The rest of it looks like another nail which is bent over.

Try making his letter shape with your thumb and fingers, holding them like this.

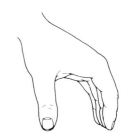

Now put your hand over your **nose** and press it against your face – say '**Nnaughty Nnnick**' a few times, slowly, until you can feel Naughty Nick's funny '**nnn**' sound going through your **nose**. This is the sound Naughty Nick makes in words.

Create in 3-D: can, man

Select four children to be Clever Cat, Annie Apple, Naughty Nick and Munching Mike.

Create 'ca...nnn', 'ca...n', 'can'. When they have discovered the word **can,** have the **c** and **a** children link the three letters together by respectively putting their hands on the **a** and **n** child's shoulders in a confirming gesture.

Compare the three children and your **can** flashcard to confirm the word.

Go on to create/discover **man** by replacing Clever Cat with Munching Mike. Confirm with an arm link and flashcard **man**.

Compare **man** and **Hairy Hat Man** flashcards, discussing small and capital **M**. Have the children put hands to noses again to make the '**nnn**' sound vibrate while they listen to themselves pronouncing **man**. Have them compare '**mmm**' with mouth shut and '**nnn**' sound in the nose, noticing that they always finish saying **man** with their mouth open so the sound will go through their nose.

Write Naughty Nick's Letter

Air Trace

Finger Trace

Handwriting Verse

Listen and Write Sheet

Involve Parents

Capital N

Remember how lots of Letterland people and animals begin important words by taking a deep breath and becoming bigger? Naughty Nick should do the same too, but the naughty fellow says 'No I won't!' Instead he does his own special trick. He starts important words with three big nails. You can see them here in his own name, **N**aughty **N**ick.

Have children with names starting with **N** make name paintings. If anyone has **nn** in their names, tell them that one **n** is Naughty Nick and the other is his next-door neighbour – Naughty Nicola. A picture code card for Naughty Nicola and an explanation of her special role in words can be found in Main Pack.

Write **no** on the board.

What does Naughty Nick like to say when he should be saying yes? Instead he says ...?

Point to the word **no**, for the children to read. Then erase it.

Code Sheet 9: nN

Follow the general instructions and the points below.

Oral naughty but nice   nails/noisy   are his hands clean?
    neighbour   nosy   numbers/one/seven/nine/ten

Picture Coding   Colour hollow **N**'s light green. Add nails. Overwrite dotted **n**'s in light green. Add Nick's head in dark green outline.

Revision   Re-read code sheets 1–4 and 7–8. Listen to and code Naughty Nick's letter, or just overwrite in green.

Important Little Word: in

The much used word **in** now comes into circulation. Point out how Naughty Nick likes making his funny '**nnn**' sound in **in**.

You can use your flashcards for **is it in ...?** and **it is in ...** to play 'Hide the Thimble' holding up the right card as you speak.

First Dictionary

Award **n** stickers. Do not add **no** until after STEP 12 (**oO**). Add **can, man, ant, hand** and **in** on the relevant pages.

Make Spelling Pictures

See the scope and sequence chart. Revise Sammy at the end in **ants** and **hands**.

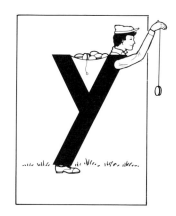

Yellow Yo-yo Man

The 15 words listed below represent the Yellow Yo-yo Man's few chances to make his own sound in words, because as soon as **y** moves into a medial or final position, this semi-vowel sounds quite different. (In Letterland terms he puts down his yo-yos to make other letters' sounds for them instead.) See '**Y**' section of the Main Pack for the relevant stories.

yard	yes	young
year	yesterday	your
years	yet	you're
yell	you	yours
yellow	you'll	yourself

The best place to meet this enthusiastic fellow is in the words **yes, yellow** and **yo-yos**.

Ⓟ Flashcards

Prepare flashcards. Colour the yo-yo's on the Picture Code Card for **y**. Also have your **no** flashcard to hand.

The Yo-yo Man's Shape

The next person for you to meet in Letterland is a good friend of Mr I's called the Yellow Yo-yo Man.

The children in Letterland can always tell when the Yo-yo Man is coming because the first thing he does is yell out,

> 'Yo-yos for sale.
> Yellow yo-yos,
> Yes, yes, yes!'

(Hold up the plain side of your **y** card.)

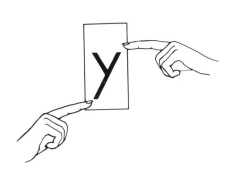

Can you picture the Yo-yo Man's head here, and his feet here? Which way will he be going?

(Elicit 'In the reading direction', and re-read your Reading Direction sign.)

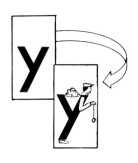

What colour will the Yellow Yo-yo Man's yo-yos be?

(Turn to the Pictogram side.)

Can you see where he carries his yellow yo-yos in his sack on his back? (Elicit 'yes'.)

What did you say? (Pretend you can't hear. Elicit a bigger 'yes'.)

Yes! And **yes** is just what the Yellow Yo-yo Man yells.

> 'Yo-yos for sale.
> Yellow yo-yos,
> Yes, yes, yes!'

The Yo-yo Man's Sound

Write **yo-yos** on the board, and **yes, yes, yes**. Picture code only the **y** in the first **yes**.

Here you can see the Yo-yo Man's letter twice in the word **yo-yos**. And here he is again at the beginning of **yes**.

If you want to discover what sound the Yo-yo Man makes in these words *start* to say 'yo-yos'. 'Yyyyy...'

Have the children prolong the '**yyy**' sound, then have them read **yes** very slowly and repeat '**Yyyyyes, yyyyes, yyyyes**'.

Hold up your **yes** flashcard and point out the **y** and the **s** sounds. Add your **no** flashcard for swift recognition. Then hold up the **yo-yos** flashcard, again pointing out the **y** and **s** sounds. Hide your flashcards behind your back and bring them out one at a time for the children to identify swiftly.

Write the Yo-Yo Man's Letter

Air Trace

Finger Trace

Listen and Write Sheet

Handwriting Verse

Involve Parents

Note. Teachers who prefer the rounded **y**-shape can describe small **y** as the Yo-yo Man kneeling while he rests his sack on the line.

Be the Yo-yo Man

The best place to play-act being the Yo-yo Man is out of doors so that the children can all yell out,

'Yyyyellow yyyyo-yyyyos for sale!'
'Yyyes, yyes, yyes.'

Some can take turns being 'youngsters' coming to buy the yo-yos, saying 'Yes please' and 'A yellow one please.'
(If you want to emphasise the slope of **y** for handwriting purposes have the children try standing on a slant too!)
Sing the **y** song on page 158.

Costume Box

Add yellow yo-yos and make yellow caps with yellow visors for young Yo-yo men to wear.

3-D Words: yes, yet

You can use your Eddy Elephant Picture Code Card to help make these two words even though you have not yet done STEP 15!

Wall Frieze: aA – zZ

Complete your alphabet wall frieze if you have not done so already by revealing the **w–z** and **W–Z** section.

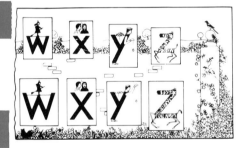

Capital Y

While the children look at **y** and **Y** explain as follows:

Many letters take a deep breath and get bigger to start an important word or name. Well, so does the Yellow Yo-yo Man. But he also does something else as well. You've seen how full his yo-yo sack is on this card, haven't you? All those yo-yos make quite a heavy load. This is why in most words you will see the Yellow Yo-yo Man resting his sack on the line. This makes him rather low down.

So when he is going to start an important word – like his own name – he quickly empties some yo-yos so he can step lightly up on to the line!

Point to the lighter load in the capital letter on the wall frieze, to reinforce this fact.

Yellow Yo-yo Man

yellow

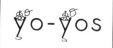

Yo-yos

Have the children study and compare the **y** and **Y** positions on your flashcards, and later in this STEP on Code Sheet 10.

The Yo-Yo Man in Names

Some children will realise that they have 'the Yo-yo Man's letter' in their names, but not his usual sound. So let them use the appropriate picture coding (yellow sack but not yo-yos) and a box inside their names. Promise stories later.

Code Sheet 10: yY

Oral his yo-yos yell to sell   youngsters love yo-yos   yes?
  your yo-yo how young is...? yards of string   yes!

Picture Coding Overwrite all plain and hollow **y**'s in thick yellow. Add head, sack, yo-yos and feet in pencil.

The Word 'Yes' Explain **yes/no** choices. These will recur on most future sheets. Ring the correct choice and cross out the incorrect one.

Revision Do *not* re-read earlier sheets as they contain final **y**'s. (The Yo-yo Man never sells yo-yos at the end of words!) Instead, have the children discover and code some or all these letters **a, m, n, i, s, d** and **hH** on the **yY** sheet.

First Dictionary

Award **y** sticker. Place on page 24 or 25 of the children's exercise books (you may want to place **x** and **y** on the same page).

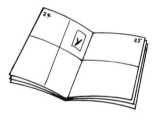

Note. For an explanation of the Yo-Yo Man's role in the word '**you**', see page 129.

Follow up

Make a large Yo-yo Man with a cloth sack so paper yo-yos can be taken in and out. (This will also be useful later when the other sounds of **y** are studied in the Main Pack.)

Make action sentences. **Add a yo-yo**
          Add 2 yo-yos
          Add 3 yo-yos, etc.

The Yo-yo Man yells 'yippee' when he sells a yo-yo.

STEP 11

Golden Girl
& her Go-car

The only Pictograms showing letters facing *against* the reading direction are **g, q** and **z**. Each has its own special explanation. This STEP features Golden Girl.* You also have a second **g** Picture Code Card with Golden Girl's lively grandmother on it. She is 'Go Go Granny' (also 'Granny Greengloves'), useful for spelling words such as **egg** at this stage. (Her vital role in predicting when to spell verbs with **gg** is explained fully in the Main Pack.)

Ⓟ Flashcards

 go   going  gone Golden Girl

Golden Girl's Letter Shape

There is a **garden** in Letterland where the **grass** is as **green** as green can be. This garden is full of **gaily** coloured flowers, and in it there is also a garden swing. The swing looks quite different from other garden swings you may have seen. This swing looks like this. (Show plain side of **g** card.) It belongs to a girl called Golden Girl. Here is how she looks when she sits in it.

Show Pictogram side of card. Show both plain and picture sides again and have several children identify on the plain letter where they saw the girl's head, her body, her legs and which is the part of the swing where she sits. Did they notice which way she faces? Elicit: '*Not* in the Reading Direction'.

Explain that Golden Girl is normally a very **good girl**. Explain, too, that she knows it's important for *everyone* in Letterland to face in the Reading Direction so they can see what letter is going to come next in a word. Yet whenever she **gets into her garden swing** she faces the wrong way! What is the matter with her?

Accept possible explanations. Then discuss how the movement of a swing can make your stomach feel funny.

Well, Golden Girl's stomach never feels funny when she's in her garden swing. Instead, her *head* feels funny. As soon as she starts to swing she **gets giddy**. So she swings round and faces the wrong way. That is why she is looking back instead of looking ahead in the Reading Direction. What a problem!

* Also, as from 1992 edition, known as 'Green Girl' because she loves gardening and cares for the environment.

81

Golden Girl's Sound (Hard g)

The hard **g** is emphasised in the Starter Pack. A story link in the Main Pack will explain soft **g**.

Maybe getting giddy explains why Golden Girl makes a funny **gurgling** sound when she is sitting in her garden swing. This is the sound she makes: '**g..,g..,g..,g..,g...**' She looks quite happy, though. Maybe she is just **giggling**.

All make her **g..,g..,g...** sound. Avoid 'guh' but do not whisper, as that will produce Clever Cat's sound instead!

Write Golden Girl's Letter

Air Trace

Finger Trace

Handwriting Verse

Listen and Write Sheet

Involve Parents

Capital G

The very different shape of capital **G** needs some emphasis. In Letterland terms it is Golden Girl's Go-Car (Go-Cart, as from 1992 edition).

Right next to Golden Girl's **garden gate** there is a **garage**. In it, Golden Girl keeps her **Go-Car**. Her Go-Car is special because it doesn't have to go on roads, like cars in *our* land. In Letterland, her Go-Car **glides** along just above the ground. This means she can even drive round her garden over the **green, green grass** without spoiling it.

Her Go-Car makes a gurgling **g..,g..,g...** sound as it glides. It sounds just like Golden Girl's **g..,g..,g...** sound. But it *could* be the **green gas** inside it gurgling instead, because green gas is what makes her Go-Car go!

All make the **g..,g..,g...** sound of her Go-Car.

3-D Words: gas, did, dig

Follow up with these routines as needed.

Slow-Speak

Play-Act

Sing Song

Quick Dash

Code Sheet 11: gG

Oral gold/golden   green glasses   glide/gliding
      green gas/grass   goggles/glare   get giddy/dizzy

Picture Coding   A stick girl will do, in light green. Overwrite
g's in dark green. Ring **yes**. Ignore the slightly different sound
of **g** in **...ing** at this stage (see Code Sheet 33).

Revision   Re-read Code Sheet 5:**mM** to code the word
magnet only. (Leave the coding of **-ing** in Munching Mike until
you have taught **-ng**.) Select any sheets for the children to re-
read, stressing fluency now that the Code Sheet vocabulary is
becoming more and more familiar.

First Dictionary

Award **g** sticker. Place on page 7. Add the word **gas** .

Follow Up Suggestions

- Create a garden in your classroom.
- Grow cress in a **g**-shape.
- Display different kinds of grasses.
- Display other things beginning with **g** – Golden Girl's glasses,
  winter gloves, garden gloves, etc.
- Make models of goats, geese, goslings, green grapes, etc.
- Collect green objects, or even create a greenhouse.
- Create a collage showing Golden Girl going in her Go-Car
  towards her garden swing.
- A series of pictures might also show her 'going, going, gone!'
  in her Go-Car.

Revision: Short a and i

3-D Words: had, handstand

You will need the letters **a,d,h,n,s,t** to make the words **had, hand, sand, stand, handstand**.

Sequence three children together to make **had**.
Introduce Naughty Nick (hoping nobody will notice him sneaking in between the apple and duck) to make **hand**.

Sequence four more children together to make **sand**. (More headbands will be needed for this.)

To discover the nine-letter word **handstand** position the two sets of four children so that the others can read **hand** and **sand** as separate words. Then have Ticking Tom come ticking along, standing on his tiptoes, to stand between Sammy and Annie Apple, to see what word he can help them to make. After the children have discovered that it is **stand**, bunch the two groups together so that they can see how all nine letters together make the word **handstand**!

3-D Words: hot hat, in/on, etc

● **Vowel substitution: a,h,i,n,s,t**
Let the children discover what words they can make when Annie Apple and and Impy Ink swap places...and change back again.
hat...hit, has...his, sat...sit, tan...tin

● **Vowel and consonant substitution: a,d,d,i,m,s,t.**
Let the children try changing any one letter and see how long a sequence they can make:
dad...did...hid...hit...hat...has...had...ham...

Other Revision Suggestions

● **Oral Game: 'I'm thinking of a thing ...'**
Revise Impy Ink's sound using a capital I this time, writing on the board: **Is it, Is it in**.

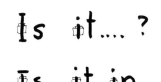

Appoint a child to think of a thing. Ask suitable questions to gain the answer to the chosen item, pointing to your **Is it** flashcard at the beginning of each one, e.g.

Is it big?   **Is it thin?**
Is it little?   **Is it sticky?**
Is it pink?   **Is it silly?**

Or, point to your **Is it in** flashcard for questions like these:

Is it in this school?   **Is it in a box?**
Is it in this room?   **Is it in a desk?**

The winner thinks of a new 'thing' and the game begins again.

● Practise action sentences.
● Practise Picture Code Card word building.
● Let the parents support and commend the children's reading at home by sending some of the first 11 Code Sheets home, to be read and returned the next day.

Note: Long Vowels as 'Vowel Men'

It is difficult to make the conventional terms 'long' and 'short' vowels meaningful to young ears. A more child oriented way to explain the 'long' vowels is to call them "Mr A, Mr E," etc. The label 'Mr' then operates as a conceptual organiser. By explaining that 'Vowel Men' appear at special times to say their names in words, you simplify for children the otherwise complicated dual-function of the vowels.

Gender Bias? Why 'Mr'? Is this a case of inadvertent gender bias? No, the reason for the choice is intensely practical. At this early stage your instruction language needs to be entirely unambiguous and simple.

Mixed labels (e.g. Mr A, Mrs or Ms E, etc.) would suggest a mix of functions. A better strategy would be to fix on one term (e.g. all 'Mr', all 'Mrs' or all 'Ms'). It happens that all the male references - Mr / man / men / he / him / his - are easy words for children to master, whereas Mrs / Ms / woman / women / ladies / girls / she / her / hers are all orthographically more complex. It is also easier for a child to isolate the long vowel sound in the phrases 'Mr A', 'Mr E' etc. than in any phrase containing an **s** just ahead of the long vowel, as in 'Mrs A' ("Missus-say"), 'Miss E' ("Miss-cee"), 'Mrs I' ("Mizz-zigh"). Finally, children find it simpler and less cluttered to draw a stick man than a stick woman to identify any long vowel within a word.

To the child who asks, "Why are **a, e, i, o,** and **u** all men?", you may like to offer a story explanation along the lines that "The 5 Vowel Men were the first settlers in Letterland. They came first to make sure that it was a safe and happy place to bring their families."

Oscar Orange & Mr O

When you teach this STEP, introduce both short and long sounds (as with **a** and **i**) but stress the short vowel sound. Reserve coding long **o** words to a few, small, high usage words at this stage (chiefly **no, go, so** and for names such as Joseph and Joan). Later Code Sheet 30 brings in more long **o** words.

Ⓟ Mural and Flashcards

Prepare an orange tree mural and these flashcards.

| Ⓞscar Ⓞrange | ⓞrange | hⓞt |
| lots and lots of | ⓞranges | ⓞn tⓞp |

Also prepare and hand out some plain **o**'s for the children to picture code and later stick on the orange tree. Show the children your Picture Code Card and, while they colour in their oranges, explain that, just as there are special apples in Letterland, there are also special juicy oranges to eat – and special *talking* oranges. The *talking* oranges say **ŏ** in words.

Talking Oranges (Short o)

Refer to your Picture Code Card.

Not all oranges grow in Letterland. Why? Because Letterland is not very **hot**, and oranges need **lots and lots** of hot sun to grow properly. So most of them are brought to Letterland by boat from other lands where there is lots of hot sunshine.

The orange tree we have here is one of the very few orange trees that grow in Letterland even though Letterland is **not hot**. The only oranges that can talk are the oranges that grow **on top**. Have you coloured in your talking oranges? Let's hear them say **ŏ** then.

Choose children to place their oranges on the top of the tree. Choose first any children with clear **ŏ** sounds in their names.

Pop your orange on the tree, (Jŏhnny). Pop it on top, where it will get as much hot sun as possible. Now you pop your orange on top, (Dŏtty), etc.

86

When there are no children's names left with short **o**, say to all the rest of the group:

Come on, let's pop lots and lots of oranges on the tree – right on the top.

The oranges should be detachable so that the children can hold them up to sing the song on page 157. At the last line place your Mr O card (small **o**) over your Oscar Orange card, and have the children put down their oranges and point to your Mr O card as you show it. Say no more about Mr O until you have consolidated your short **o** teaching.

 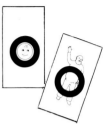

 lots and lots of

hot

on top

oranges

Oscar Orange and His Sound

We don't know the names of all of the Letterland oranges, but we do know the name of this one. (Show Oscar Orange card.) He is Oscar Orange, and he says ŏ in lots and lots of words.

Hold up the **lots and lots of** flashcard. Have the children listen for Oscar's ŏ sound as you read the card.

Oscar Orange can say ŏ in **lots** and he can say ŏ in **hot**. He can say ŏ in **on** and he can say ŏ in **top**. And of course he says ŏ in the word **orange**!

Show the **orange** and **oranges** flashcards. Have the children compare the two and help you choose the plural flashcard to place on top of the orange tree mural. Add the **on top** flashcard to read: **oranges on top**.

Write Oscar Orange's Letter

Air Trace

Handwriting Verse

Listen and Write Sheet

Involve Parents

Capital O (Short Sound)

Explain capital **O** roughly along these lines.

To start an important word Oscar Orange uses the same trick as quite a few other letters. He just takes a deep breath and becomes bigger. Who else uses this trick among those we have met so far?

Revise all capital letters already covered. (The deep breath trick so far applies to **c,t,s** and in a special way to **y**.) Discuss capital **a,d,m,i,n** and **g** as well.

3-D Words: hot hat, in/on, etc

Re-cap on the short vowel sounds **ă, ĭ** and **ŏ**.

Have four children help you discover what happens when Oscar Orange swaps places with Annie Apple or Impy Ink.

**hot...hat...hit
in...on...an**

You can also ask the children to experiment with the Picture Code Cards to see whether they will get a real word or not, e.g. dig...dog...dag?

Code Sheet 12: oO

Oral	top notch orange	on top	drop
	oblong box	not on top	bottom

Picture Coding An orange dot inside each short **o** will do. Adding Oscar's face is optional. As always, stress listening because the correct picture coding might be an orange *or* (now or later) a stick man. (See code sheet 30.)

Revision Re-read code sheets 5 – 8. Find and code Oscar Orange.

First Dictionary

Award **o** sticker. Place on page 15. Leave room for the children to add a bearded stick man after they have learnt to code Mr O. Add the word **on** now.

Mr O, the Old Man

If the children seem quite happy coping with the presence of Mr A and Mr I in a limited number of words, they should be able to handle the idea of another Vowel Man who also pops into words sometimes to say his name. Ask which Vowel Men they have met so far. Briefly discuss Mr A, **owner** of the apples, and Mr I who sells ice cream and ink.

Mr O, the Old Man is a good friend of Mr A and Mr I. He is also the **oldest** Vowel Man of all. Everyone is glad that Mr O lives in Letterland, because without him there would hardly be any oranges at all. Remember, Letterland is too cold for most oranges to grow there. That is why Mr O, the Old Man, brings whole boat loads of oranges from **over** the **ocean** to Letterland.

He sells quite a few of them, but he does *not* sell the talking oranges like Oscar. Instead he spends most of his time popping oranges like Oscar into lots and lots and lots of words which need an **ŏ** sound in them.

88

This job keeps him **so** busy that he **only** has time to appear in words himself at special times. Let's keep a sharp look out in case we come across him in some words. He particularly likes turning up in quite *small* words.

These small words are **no, go** and **so**. You will already have treated **no** and **go** as sight words on the **n** and **g** Code Sheets. Now the children can code them on Sheet 30 (Mr O) if you judge the timing to be right. Photocopy Sheet 30 excluding the other long **o** words, if you wish, at this stage.

Code Sheet 30: oO

Oral old/oh so old   still full of go   wise old so-and-so
over the ocean   knows all there is to know

Picture Coding Guide the children's listening. Keep asking 'orange, or Mr O himself this time?' Code stick man in any bright colour. Include beard.

Revision Find and code Mr O on Sheets 6, 9 and 11, in **telephone, no, go** and (for sharp eyes) in **Golden**. (Also 20 **Hello**.)

3-D Words: go, so, no

Reinforce the spelling of these words with the Picture Code Cards. Also prepare a poster listing these three little high-usage words. Read through it together regularly until they become easy sight vocabulary. Have the children make their own versions of the poster for their folders.

3-D Words: on, no

Choose a good time, later still, to compare **on** and **no** in 3-D, on the Picture Code Cards and by making spelling pictures yourself of both words, which the children can then copy.

Nodding Game

Use flashcards for **nod:yes** and **nod:no** to play a game.

- Choose a child to stand up in front of the others with the two cards to choose from within easy reach.
- Ask any questions, e.g. 'Is it raining?'
  'Does Carlo have black hair?'
  'Are you hungry?'
- The child must select the right nodding reaction, hold up the appropriate flashcard for the group to read, and respond with the correct nod.

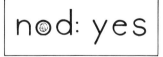

Oscar's Little Brother

Your 50 picture code cards include a small card for Oscar's little brother. He is Letterland's version of the irregular **o** in **brother, mother, other**, etc. This **o** always crops up early in reading and writing because it occurs in so many common words. Introduce this bothersome but lovable little br**o**ther whenever you think fit.

No words containing Oscar's little brother occur on Code Sheets 1 – 34, but you may like to start a collection as soon as examples (e.g. **come**) occur, especially where spelling is concerned.

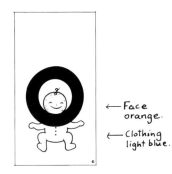

←Face orange.

←Clothing light blue.

Present this bothersome brother as always willing to *try* and say 'o' like Oscar, but his sound always comes out as '**u**' instead, no matter how hard he tries.

Code Sheet 35: Oscar's Little Brother

Oral bothersome done up (compare vowels)
lovable   undone (compare vowels)

Picture Coding   Orange face. Blue baby clothes. Children who already know the short **u** sound might like to give him a tiny little umbrella to signal that he always makes Uppy Umbrella's sound by mistake.

other love
brother
mother

First Dictionary

The best place for this irregular **o** is the inside back cover of each child's first dictionary. Collect words here with Oscar's little brother both at the beginning and inside words. See page 141.

Rhodri

Lilo

Shamus

This is Ⓞscar's Little Brⓞther.

dⓞne ủp

ủndⓞne

Fireman Fred

Introduce Fireman Fred as a character who is both fierce, when he is fighting fires, and friendly in his free time. He is fond of children, fond of fishing and fond of food. After you have developed his character, encourage the children to add their own ideas about him.

In this STEP you will also be introducing Fireman Frank, Fred's friend and fellow fireman, who always sets **off** to fight fires with Fireman Fred.

When colouring your **ff** Picture Code Card give the firemen different colour skins so both of these heroes look like different nationalities (perhaps groups of children in your class).

Ⓟ Flashcards

Fireman Fred's Shape

Hold up your Fireman Fred card, showing the Pictogram side, and introduce him along these lines. (Use Frank first, if you prefer, but be consistent.)

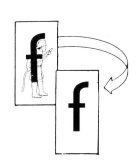

Here's Fireman Fred who runs the **fire station** in Letterland. He and his **fellow firemen** are the **fastest fire fighters** you can **find** anywhere.

What is Fireman Fred wearing? Look, he has a **fine fire helmet**. He has a **fine fire-proof** coat, and he has **fine fire-proof** boots.

What do you think Fireman Fred uses in his hose for putting out fires? It's not water – it's something **frothy** and white. It's **foam**! (Discuss the meaning of foam if necessary.)

Fireman Fred's Sound

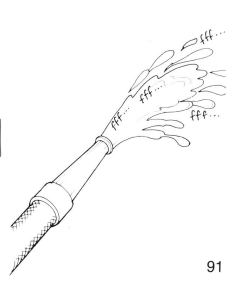

As Fireman Fred's foam **forces** its way out of the hose it makes a **funny, fizzy** sort of sound like this: '**fff**'.

(This is a *voiceless* sound so make sure that the children do not produce it with voice ('fffuh').

Whenever you see Fireman Fred in a word you will hear that fizzy '**fff**' sound as the foam flows from the firehose.

Discuss fire-fighting and fire prevention, and generally involve the figure of Fireman Fred in any Safety First work. Explain that in Letterland schools he has already told all the children about Safety First. That is how he makes sure that there will be very few fires to fight in Letterland.

Write Fireman Fred's Letter

Air
Trace

Handwriting
Verse

Listen
and Write

Involve
Parents

Capital F

Like some letters you have met so far (point to the lower half of your wall frieze), Fireman Fred takes a deep breath to start an important word. In this case, his letter becomes a little bigger *and* sharper as well.

More about Fireman Fred

Encourage the children to build up their own image of Fireman Fred by associating alliterative words. You can help by offering choices, as shown below. As they learn to pick words beginning with Fred's sound, they will discover how much more they already 'know' about Fireman Fred than they thought. Soon, instead of you asking them, they will be *telling* you.

Encourage this creative contribution from the children. It will be an important component in making Letterland their own – as well as keeping your own teaching fresh each year.

In his **free time**, what do you think Fireman Fred likes best? Hunting or **fishing**?

What do you think Fireman Fred's **favourite food** might be? Spinach soup or **fresh fish**?

What is his **favourite** dessert? Coconut cake or **fruit flan**?

Where does Fireman Fred live? In a house on a hill or the **fourth floor** of the **fire station**?

What is his room number? It could be 4,5,15,40,50,54,55 or even 555! (Decide together on **55**.)

Is Fireman Fred a bad tempered man or a nice **friendly fireman**?

Revise what you now all know, getting the alliterative sentences onto the children's lips.

Do we like Fireman Fred? Yes we do!

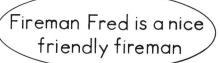

Fireman Fred is a nice friendly fireman

3-D Words

fat   cat   cats   if   gift   gifts

More words are listed on your scope and sequence chart.

3-D Word Copying

Have the children write down **fat** by copying the letters on three children.

Slow Speak

Use 'slow-speak' to help the children spell by ear **fat cat** and **fat cats**. 'Ffffaat, Caaa...t (Avoid cuh..at!) Let them also try **if, fit, gift,** and **fog** if you judge they are ready.

Blends

Use your Picture Code Cards to practise consonant/vowel/consonant blends with these words.

fa(t)	**ha(t)**	**ma(t)**	**sa(d)**	**ha(d)**
fi(t)	**hi(t)**	**mi(ss)**	**si(t)**	**hi(d)**
	hi(ss)			

Code Sheet 13: fF and ff

Oral   flames, fire   flicker, flare up   fearless
         off in a flash   flood the fire   fine fellows

Picture Coding   Listen, overwrite **f**'s in dark blue. Draw Fireman Fred in orange. Discuss **ff** as a shared sound. Later compare/contrast **off** with **of** on Code Sheet 18 (**v**). Compare **I am** with **I'm**. Compare **Fred** and **Frank**. Code **d** and **k** to emphasise the difference. Add one fireman to four firemen to make ... five!

Revision   Re-read Code Sheets 3 and 7 (**d** and **s**). Code **ff** in **daffodil**.

First Dictionary

Award **f** sticker and place it on page 6. The words **fit, fat** and **fog** can now be added.

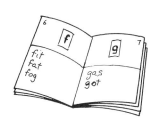

Fireman Fred and Fireman Frank: ff

Discuss how fire fighting is usually a job for a whole team of firemen. Try to find out how many firemen are on your local fire station team.

Fireman Fred has lots of **fellow firemen** who can help him put out fires. Often they work in two's. This is how they go about it in Letterland.

Whenever Fireman Fred sets **off** to fight a fire he *always* sets off with his best friend **Fireman Frank**. This is why you will always see them together in the word **off**.

Off is an important word – it is on switches, TV knobs, etc. Discuss this with the children.

Count buttons on the firemen's uniforms to discover which numbers begin with Fred and Frank's sound (**four** down the **front** and one on the cuff makes ... **five**!

Find other words with double **ff** (e.g. **huff, puff**.) Can the children find STAFF on the staffroom door?

Spelling Pictures: if, off, etc

Suggest the following: **fat cat(s), on/off, sad cat** and **sad Sam**. Also make a large spelling picture of the word **if** to add to the 'Important Little Words' list in STEP 8 **il** (see page 70).

Play-Act Being Firemen

Do not try to memorise all the alliterative words in these miming suggestions. Just include as many words beginning with **f** as you can conveniently use.

Stand up, everybody, and let's all be **firemen** just like Fireman Fred and Fireman Frank. This wall behind us is a page in Letterland, so **face forward**, looking in the Reading Direction, just like them, and grab your **firehose** in your **fists**.

Can you **feel** the **foam flowing** through it? It **forces** its way out of the nozzle. What kind of sound does it make as it **floods** the **flames? It goes fff, fff, fff**! Now the leaping **flames** are **falling**. In a **flash the fire fizzles** out! Not a **flicker** left! You've done a **fine** job, just like Fireman Fred and Fireman Frank. Well done, children – in **fact, fantastic**!

Quick Dash

You have 12 cards to practise now: **a, c, d, f, ff, g, h, i, m, n, s, ss** and **t**. Can the children reel off the sounds only? From the plain sides only? Can they respond swiftly to the character name flashcards too? And some of the spelling pictures on the walls?

94

Poor Peter

Poor Peter is a pup with a problem. Most children's response to this character is one of fond sympathy, perhaps because nearly everyone (children and adults alike) are sensitive in some way about themselves. Poor Peter's problem is his ears which are long and floppy. Everybody else likes his long, floppy ears, but not Poor Peter. He hates the way they droop. You also have a second **p** Picture Code Card for Poor Peter's pal, Poor Patsy, whose ears droop too. Use one at each end of the word **pup** in 3-D word making. (When and why **pp** may be needed in a word is fully explained in the Main Pack.)

Ⓟ Flashcards

| pat | puppy | poor | Poor Peter |

Poor Peter's Shape

The emphasis on droopy ears is, of course, a strategy for emphasising the down stroke of **p**, in contrast to the **b** and **d** **shapes**. Entrust the children with the job of cheering Peter up by **always stroking him properly**. They may like to make droopy ears with **pale** brown **patches** to attach to the headbands and so **pretend** to be him. Then get them to **practise** stroking down each other's ears – responding of course by looking **pleased**.

Poor Peter's Sound

Poor Peter not only has a problem with his ears, but to make matters worse this poor puppy has a second problem. He can't bark! The only sound he can make is a funny little, very quiet '**p...**' sound. He makes this sound by shutting his mouth and blowing through his lips. (Have the children do the same. Make sure they *don't* add voice.)

The reason that Poor Peter can't bark is that he is a Letterland puppy. So naturally he makes a special sound instead of barking the way ordinary dogs in *our* land do. He should really be **pleased**, and **proud** of his special sound. But he's not (Encourage the children to feel protective towards him.) It is important to remember that **p** is a voiceless consonant, so *any pause* between it and the next letter will distort its sound (puh). Use the Blending Verse (page 42) and Audio Tape to sing it.

Write Poor Peter's Letter

Air
Trace

Handwriting
Verse

Listen
and Write

Involve
Parents

Sing

Play
Act

Action
Sentence

Capital P

In most words Poor Peter rests his chin on the line, but for capital **P** he takes a deep breath and then does his own special trick. He **pops up**! He hopes, with this trick, to make his ears pop up, too, and *stay* up. Sadly, he is always disappointed. They still droop even after he has popped up. Poor, Poor Peter! But he keeps on trying all the same, every time he can begin an important word. (Compare the position of **p** on your **poor** and **Poor Peter** flashcards, and on Code Sheet 14: **pP**.)

3-D Words: pat, pot, spot, spots, dots

The Scope and Sequence Chart provides an ever-increasing number of words. Use more and more for setting out on the Picture Code Cards, for slow-speak spelling, and making spelling pictures.

Code Sheet 14: pP

Oral poor/no money happy/pleased pepper spots pity him
poor/unhappy funny/playful plump pup patches

Picture Coding   Overwrite broken-line **p**'s in black or purple. Keep picture coding simple. Just head, ears and dot for nose is enough, preferably in pink (Poor Peter's favourite colour). Explain the function of the question mark symbol (printed in grey to denote a silent symbol).

Revision   Re-read Code Sheets 1 – 5, as well as Sheet 12 (**c, a, d, h, m** and **o**). Find and code (or just overwrite **p**'s in pink).

First Dictionary

Award **p** sticker. Place on page 16. Some or all words beginning with **p** listed on the 3-D section of the Scope and Sequence Chart can now be added.

Follow-up: Paint a Puzzle

Paint a picture of Poor Peter. Turn it into a Poor Peter Puzzle by cutting it up and putting it back together again!

Kicking King

The **k** sound occurs relatively infrequently at the beginning of words. The Letterland explanation for such rare appearances is a purely practical one. The Kicking King finds there is not much room for a good kick at the start of a word, or in the middle for that matter. This is why you see Letterland's ruler so often at the end of words instead, where there is plenty of room to kick!

In terms of character, the words **kind** and **kick** create useful alliterative associations for Letterland's king. He is a kindly monarch, and he is very popular because he is a keen sportsman – the best kicker in the kingdom.

Ⓟ Flashcards

Kicking King's Shape

Hold up the Pictogram side of your Picture Code Card.

Not every country has a king, but *Letterland* has one, and he is a good, **kind king**, so everyone likes him. He is also very good at sports. He can kick a ball farther than anyone else in all his **kingdom**. You will often see him practising his kick in words. Look for a tall letter with one arm up and one leg forward in just the right place for a good **kick**.

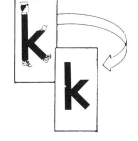

Turn the card to the plain side and have the children indicate and discuss where the king's body fits in.

Write the Kicking King's Letter

Air Trace

Handwriting Verse

Listen and Write

Involve Parents

Sing

Play Act

Action Sentence

97

Capital K

Sometimes the Kicking King looks bigger at the beginning of words. That's because he takes a deep breath. Who else have we met so far who does that getting-bigger trick to start important words? (Discuss.)

Show how, in the case of the king, it is mainly his arm and leg that become bigger when he takes a deep breath.

Kicking King's Sound

Let's discover Kicking King's sound. Just *start* to say 'Kicking King'. You can hear his sound best if you *whisper* 'Kicking King'. Whisper it slowly and carefully and you should hear his sound in the back of your throat, three times: **k...k...k...**

Examine your **Kicking King** flashcard so the children can see him appearing three times as well as hearing him. Remind them that, like all Letterland people and animals, the Kicking King can be in several places at once!

Compare C and K Sounds

Can you think of someone else in Letterland who makes a '**k**' sound, just like the King?

Have everyone whisper 'Clever Cat' and then 'Kicking King' so that they hear/*feel* the identical sound in their throats.

Clever Cat is very pleased and proud to share the same sound as the Kicking King. And of course she loves to watch him kick. That is why you will always see her sitting carefully just behind the king's ba**ck** at the end of the word **kick**.

Discuss this point again later on Code Sheet 15: **kK**. Ways of predicting when to use **c, k** or **-ck** in spelling come later (in the Main Pack). At present your aim is limited to shape and sound recognition and correct letter formation.

Code Sheet 15: kK

Oral

| king/kingdom | kind king/well loved | keen on pets |
| kind of king | keen (meaning of) | kittens/kangaroo |

Picture Coding Code **k**'s. When **king** ends a word, add a ball. Over-write broken-line **k**'s in dark blue. Point out Ticking Tess sharing the '**t**' sound and the word **ten** in **kittens**.

Revision Re-read Code Sheets 3, 6 and 8–14 (**d, t** and **i–p**). Find **k** (on some sheets). Over-write in thick blue (coding is optional).

First Dictionary

Award **k** sticker. Place on page 11. The words **kick** and **kiss** can now be added. Wait until you have taught **-ng** (below) before adding **king** and **kicking**.

The -NG Sound

This Starter Pack gives high priority to the **ng** sound for three reasons.

● First, the fact that letters often change their sounds because they 'meet in a word' needs to be understood as soon as possible.

● Second, the **ng** sound usually occurs at the *end* of words, enabling you to alert the children to look not just at the start, but also at the full length of words.

● Third, **ng** turns up often not just in common words like **bring**, **sing**, and **thing** but in thousands of words ending in **ing**. The **ng** story is given in this STEP because **ng** occurs twice in the name Kick**ing** K**ing** – an opportunity too good to miss!

Explore the word **king**. Appoint four children to form the word. Have Golden Girl face Naughty Nick (against the Reading Direction, as usual)! Confirm the Kicking King's sound at the start of the word, and Impy Ink's ĭ sound next. Then encourage the children to discover (with the help of Naughty Nick and Golden Girl), that sometimes letters make a new sound when they meet each other in a word. Explain that we don't say '**ki/nn/g**'. We say '**ki/ng**'. So what has happened to Naughty Nick and Golden Girl? Neither of them is making their usual sound! Why not?

To explain the '**ng**' sound which Naughty Nick and Golden Girl are mak**ing** in the word ki**ng** I must tell you a bit more about Naughty Nick. You might not think that such a *naughty* boy would like such a *good* girl as Golden Girl, but he does!

Naughty Nick really would like Golden Girl to be his best friend. Golden Girl hasn't said she will be yet, but even so, she is always *very* pleased to see him. In fact, they are both so pleased whenever they come face to face in a word that they start sing**ing**. Can you hear their special sing**ing** sound at the end of the word **king**?

Consonant Caper: sk While this lively song highlights the **sk** blend you can also point out the **-ing** endings in the words ski**ing** and skimm**ing**.

Write **Kicking King** on the board and help the children to discover Naughty Nick and Golden Girl singing their special '**ng**' sound at the end of **kicking** as well as at the end of K**ing**. *The -ing ending.* Point out how very often Impy Ink turns up right beside the two friends, watch**ing** them s**inging**.

Remind the children of the **ng** story casually as you come across other words containing -**ing**. Keep drawing their attention to this final syllable to encourage them to realise that end**ings** are worth notic**ing** just as much as initial letters.

3-D Words: king, sing/song, ding/dong,

Make **sing, sang, song, dig/ding, dog/dong,** etc.
More words are suggested on the Scope and Sequence chart.
Use a few for 3-D word making, others for Picture Code Card word building and slow-speak spelling.

Code Sheet 33: ing

Oral

Doing words	sitting	listening	thinking	getting up
What are	breathing	talking	blinking	standing
you doing?	looking	moving	wishing	walking

Picture Coding   Overwrite all -**ing**'s in thick red so they stand out. Code in light green, or simplify the coding by having the children box **ing** and add music notes only.

Revision   Re-read Code Sheets 5 – 15 (**m – k**) scanning for -**ing** endings. (These numbers include sheets without -**ing** endings, because the scanning practice is valuable in its own right.)

Bell Ringing Song: -ing, -ang, -ong, -ung

Listen to this song on Letterland Audio Tape No. 1 and decide when to include it in your teaching.

Make bells so you can change the ringing order for the children to read and sing. Write just the -**ing**'s in red. Write **ang, ong** and **ung** in black only.

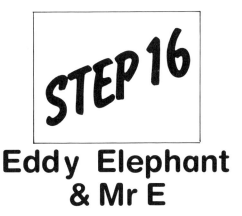

Eddy Elephant & Mr E

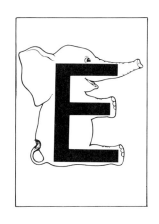

You will need three of your Picture Code Cards – those for Eddy Elephant and his master, Mr E the Easy Magic Man, plus your plain grey **e** card to represent silent **e**'s. The more advanced concept of the silent **magic e**'s (and their usefulness as signals for pronouncing the preceding vowel – e.g. tap, tape) is fully dealt with in the Main Pack. At this stage, if you need to show children how to code their names (e.g. Jane, Steve) or a common word (e.g. like, hope), use the grey silent **e** Picture Code Card. In name paintings use grey paint or write the silent **e** in dots (as though it is fading away, like its sound).

Note that **ee** coding occurs in Step 23: **Qu**.

You will be introducing Eddy Elephant as a very friendly elephant, who encourages everyone in their reading and writing by pointing his trunk in the Reading Direction.

Ⓟ Flashcards

Eddy Elephant's Shape

Start with a discussion about different kinds of pets. Lead up to this question:

*Do you know anyone who has an elephant for a pet? Well in Letterland there is a man who does. This elephant is called Eddy Elephant. (Show Pictogram side of card.) You can tell that he's a Letterland elephant because he always points his trunk in the Reading Direction, like this. (Turn card to the plain **e** side.)*

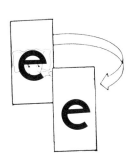

Even when you can't see Eddy Elephant's face in his letter you can still see his trunk pointing in the Reading Direction. You show me where his trunk is here.

Have several children come and touch the plain side of the card. Keep turning over to the Pictogram side to confirm their findings.

Eddy Elephant's Sound

Eddy Elephant **expects** that some of you children might be able to guess what sound he makes in words.

Have you noticed that all you have to do is *start* to say Sammy Snake's name to make his hissing sound 'Ssssammy...**Ssss**'? Or *start* to say 'Munching Mike' to make his '**Mmmm**' sound?

So if you *start* to say 'Eddy Elephant' you can discover Eddy Elephant's sound. (Elicit **ĕ**.) Yes! Eddy Elephant **enjoys** saying **ĕ** ever so much in lots of words **every** day!

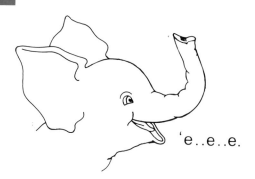

'e..e..e.

Write Eddy Elephant's Letter

Air
Trace

Handwriting
Verse

Listen
and Write

Involve
Parents

Eddy Elephant Belongs to Mr E

Here is the lucky man who has Eddy Elephant for a pet. His name is Mr E. (Show Mr E card, Pictogram side.)

Eddy Elephant feels lucky too, belonging to Mr E, because Mr E is the Easy Magic Man. He knows lots of magic tricks. All these tricks would be difficult for *you* or *me* to do, but not for Mr E. For him they are all **eeeasy**! That is why everyone calls him 'Mr E, the Easy Magic Man'.

Hold up *both* cards and allow discussion.

1

2

Play-act, Sing About Eddy Elephant

Hold up your Eddy card until the last line. Then hold up your Mr E card. Say no more about Mr E at this stage. Concentrate instead on Eddy Elephant's **ĕ** sound.

Capital E

Now, there is a special trick which Eddy Elephant has learned to do all by himself. He would like you to see it. He only does it at the beginning of names and very important words. This is what he does. (Point to capital **E** on the frieze.) He sits down on **end** and points ... not just his trunk ... but **everything** in the Reading Direction:

    his back legs,
    his front legs,
    and his trunk.

He calls this his '**Elephant-on-End**' trick.

3-D words: yes, end

Make **yes** in 3-D to reinforce easy recognition of this word on many of the Code Sheets following this STEP. For **end**, blend the **ĕ-nnn** first. Pause before you add Dippy Duck 'to *end* the word **end**'!

Silent E

Curiously, although Eddy Elephant loves making a sound to *start* the word **end**, his sound never turns up at the *ends* of words. Instead, if you **ever** see his letter at the **end** of a word it will be **empty**! So of course it will make no sound at all. Everyone in Letterland calls these **empty** letters 'silent **e**'s'. Here is a silent **e**. (Show the grey **e** card.)

Take time, either now or later, to help the children to *deduce* this fact by looking at and listening to any words encountered so far with silent **e**'s at the end.

snake   like
give live

Make sure no child puts Eddy at the end of their name. If the deed is already done, no matter. Just put their elephant in a box. Their coding will still have helped to remind them of the correct letter sequence for their name. The more accurate coding with an empty silent **e** should be used next time.

Joanne

Be Eddy Elephant

Now, I'd like you all to *be* elephants, just like Eddy Elephant. Think of the wall in front of you as a great big page and tell me which way you are going to lumber along? Which way is Eddy's trunk pointing in this picture? (Show Pictogram side and plain side of the card. Elicit, 'In the Reading Direction!')

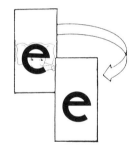

Also point to establish clockwise movement for the 'elephants' to go around the room or hall. Their arms should be clasped together for trunks, swinging loosely in front of them. They can point ahead from time to time, just like Eddy.

Let's hear Eddy Elephant's sound too. (Chorus of **ĕ** sounds.) Now stop, elephants, and let's see if you can do Eddy's '**Elephant-on-End**' trick. Sit down, slowly, just like Eddy Elephant. Stretch your hind legs out straight. Use one arm now to show where your front legs are. Use the other arm for your trunk. Is **everybody** pointing **everything** in the Reading Direction? Yes? Right, let's hear you all saying '**ĕ**' again.

'e..e..e..'   'e..e..e..'

If you happen to have a camera, take a few photographs of your children in the capital **E** position. Your camera could give you an excuse to revise other letter shapes as well. Keep these photos, and any others you may take later on. Collected together, they will make an unusual additional teaching resource, both for this and subsequent years.

Entrance and Exit Signs

Find any **exit** and **entrance** signs in the school. Discuss their meanings. Find space for an elephant house. Make signs.

Make elephant headbands so that everyone can be an elephant in a subsequent play period, **entering** and **exiting** as often as they like from the Elephant House. Let them take the headbands home, but keep one or two for the costume box.

Parent Involvement: Labelling at Home

Write out and duplicate an 'Entrance' and 'Exit' sign for each child to picture code and take home to put on their bedroom doors.

From now on suggest to parents that they help their child to select no more than three items around the house beginning with each new sound they learn and label them. Take the labels down when they bring home the next sound to learn. Stress that these labels should be treated as sight words, to practise instant recognition, but make sure no parent TESTS their child. Playful learning makes children *like* learning. Too high a parent expectation can destroy that pleasure. Their aim should be to foster an interest in words *in general*, *not* proficiency in reading these particular words.

3-D Word: ten

Use the letters **t, e, n** and **s** to explore the effects on meaning of the following changes in letter order.

ten → net → nets → nest → sent → tent → tents

Also practise vowel substitution

man → men   miss → mess

More words are listed on the Scope and Sequence Chart.

The Full Stop Dot = The End

This is a good time to draw attention to the full stop dot as a signal meaning 'end of the message'. Make sure you have included one at the end of your **on end.** flashcard. Finish the lesson by having the children read the two new flashcards.

From now on make sure you add a full stop to all your board sentences. Draw attention to them at regular intervals.

Code Sheet 16: eE

Oral   end, endings   entrance   seven/ten/eleven
             on end/The End   exit   elbow/edge

Picture Coding   Listen, overwrite broken-line **e**'s in red. Code Eddy in red. Ring **yes**.

Revision   Re-read Code Sheets 6 – 8, 10, 13 and 15 (**t, s, i, y, f** and **k**). Warn the children *not* to draw in Eddy Elephant if they cannot hear his sound (**-er** endings and silent **e**'s).

First Dictionary

Award **e** sticker. Place it on page 5. The words **end** and **egg** can be added. Leave space on the right for a stick man after you teach all about Mr E. Now you can add more **d** words too.

Spelling Pictures

Quick Dash and Action Sentences

Include both the Eddy Elephant and silent **e** cards from now on in your daily dash. You may like to ask the children to cover their mouths to emphasise silent **e**. You can also show both **e**'s plain sides and play at guessing which one has Eddy on the reverse.

Use the action sentences for practice in silent reading.

Mr E the Easy Magic Man

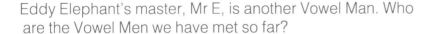

It is useful to start picture coding a few key words with stick men either now or later, but *first* link Mr E in the children's minds with the other Vowel Men.

Eddy Elephant's master, Mr E, is another Vowel Man. Who are the Vowel Men we have met so far?

Briefly review Mr A, Mr I and Mr O.

Right! Mr A collects apples in his apron. Mr I sells ink and ice cream. Mr O brings oranges from over the ocean. And these three Vowel Men are all good friends of the Easy Magic Man called Mr...? Right! Mr E! All the other Vowel Men think Mr E is very clever because he makes all his magic tricks look so **eeeasy**. Do *you* think magic tricks are **eeeasy**?

Explain that Mr E has worked so hard practising his magic tricks that they have *become* easy for him. Explain also that when he is not busy working on a new magic trick, he loves to pop into a word and say his name, just as the other Vowel Men do.

Here are two little words to look out for where you can hear Mr E saying his name, loud and clear.

Put these words on a chart and leave room to add four other words later (**we, be, she** and **the**). Apart from a few names, (e.g. Daphne, Phoebe) these six are the ONLY common words where a final **e** is not empty (silent), because Mr E himself is appearing in it. (Strictly speaking the word **the** does not qualify when pronounced quickly, but for spelling purposes it is worth grouping it with the other five.)

The Word 'see'

This word is in the high usage bracket. While **see** is easy to learn as a distinctive whole-word shape, it is also easy to picture code with Mr E and his twin brother, a second Mr E. So find a convenient time to show the children how to code **see** with drawings of two stick men side-by-side. They will soon find **ee** turning up again in STEP 23: **qu, Qu** inside the word **queen**.

This is a good time to point out that Eddy Elephant never turns up with another elephant right beside him in a word. (Elephants are too big to share one sound!) Instead Mr E says his name, loud and clear, while his twin brother quietly keeps a look-out for danger (in the form of bad people like the Wicked Witch and Robber Red – see STEPS 19 and 24).

How to Spell the Word 'they'

The word **they** has been misspelt millions of times by millions of children in every country where English is taught, and patiently (or impatiently) corrected by millions of teachers.

Introduce Mr Mean-E early on to make sure none of your children join these millions. Mr Mean-E says:

> Hee, hee, hee. I'm an <u>e</u>,
> but I say 'a' in **they**!
> I'll be glad just as long
> as you spell **they** wrong!

Let everyone make spelling pictures of **they** showing this very different **e** – *not* a relation of Mr E at all but an old scrooge, a real meany (Mean-E), instead. Challenge the children to make sure old Mr Mean-E cannot gloat over their mistake. Don't let him fool them just because he sounds exactly like Mr A in this one word. (Later add **grey**, as needed in spelling.)

Code Sheet 28: Mr E/Mr Mean-E

Photocopy this sheet excluding (**we, me,** etc) at first, if you wish, or just exclude **they** if the children are not ready yet for the whole sheet.

Picture Coding Complete the top-hatted stick man in red to confirm Mr E's sound in the six little words. Compare with the grey **e** in **these** which is silent, just as most final **e**'s are, apart from these six.

Code Mr Mean-E in red, too, but show him bent over and hobbling along with a stick.

Piedro

Mr Mean-E Song Revise the spelling of **they** and **grey** by singing and play-acting Mr Mean-E's gloating song given in Audio Tape 2B and accompanying Songbook 2B. Introduce this song now or later for **they**. Use it again later for **grey**. Still later you might substitute **obey, convey,** etc. to support more spelling.

REVISION OF STEPS 1 – 16

You have told the children 'stories' about 16 characters. Now turn the tables. Retelling stories encourages self-expression and consolidates learning. Have the children give you a character sketch of each person or animal met in Letterland so far. Help them to include as many descriptive words as possible (both alliterative and others).

Revise Handwriting Verses

Have the parents been helping with handwriting practice? Can the children now begin to read the verses?

Most verses are going to be 'readable' at this stage chiefly because the children can anticipate the words. This is all to the good, as they are (i) thinking of the message and (ii) moving their eyes along at a gentle sight-reading pace. Both are very desirable forms of reading behaviour. Gradually they will also really notice, for example, Dippy Duck at the start of the word **dot** and Ticking Tom at the other end.

Listen to the Ends of Words

Have your picture code cards and character name flashcards ready for the following letters: **c,d,e,f,g,h,j,k,m,,t,v**.

Hold up the Picture Code Cards one by one. Ask the children to say each character name, paying special attention now to the *last* sound that comes out of their mouths.

Who helps Clever Cat to finish spelling her name?

Hold up the Clever Cat flashcard and point to the plain **t**. (Answer: Ticking Tom.) Hold up Dippy Duck flashcard etc. These character names for the 12 letters above give practise in identifying final **d,k,l,m,n,s,t** and **ng**. You may like to extend this game to children's names, or spelling pictures on the wall, or to topical words which end in any of the sounds so far taught.

Revise 'in' and 'on'

Choose four or five children to come and write and code the word **in** on the board, using blue chalk for the coding. Choose four or five more children to write and code **on**, with coding in orange chalk.

Then play 'Hide the Thimble'. Write on the board:

Is it in .....?
Is it on .....?

Have the children come and point to the relevant phrase as they ask out loud what it might be *in* or *on*.

Revise -ng

Find rhyming words for the **-ing** character names.

Ticking Tom/**Kicking** King
picking/licking/sticking
clicking/pricking/tricking

Munching Mike
lunching/punching
crunching/bunching

Kicking **King**
sing(ing) sting(ing)
ding(ing) ring(ing)
ping(ing) zing(ing

Jumping Jim
bumping/dumping/pumping

Find **-ang/-ong** words

-ang	-ong
bang	bong
gang	gong
fangs	ping pong

Revise Letters in Music and Movement

Rhythmic repetition of any letter's sound, accompanied by either a simple mime gesture or dance movement and background music, provides a unique kinaesthetic and accoustic experience for each child.

Miming of six to twelve letters (no Picture Code Cards or headbands needed) can even be made worthy of a little assembly performance. For example, all children tick as lots of Tom's and Tess's slowly turn on tip-toe, arms outstretched. The audience then ticks too.

Ear-First Game: Phase 2

Play as described on page 43. Use different lists on different days. First have the children make the following cards, plain on one side, coded on the other, as before.

1. yeast	1. flying fish	1. new nest
2. tailor	2. slippery slope	2. nice neighbour
3. yellow yolk	3. swimming swans	3. golden grain
4. tall trees	4. funny fork	4. growing grass
5. table top	5. singsong	5. never, never
6. triangle	6. sausage	6. gooey glue
7. yardstick	7. forest of fir trees	7. nine needles
8. teletypewriter	8. freezing fog	8. gobbling goats
9. youngster	9. fresh flowers	9. group of girls
10. yacht	10. seven seas	10. no nonsense

For a more difficult game, mix **nN** words given here with **mM** words listed on page 63.

Revise 'Slow-Speak' Words

The 3-D word building should have led to daily 'slow-speak' spelling practise by now. If some children still find putting slow speech to paper difficult, conduct these sessions at three levels.

The children choose. They write the *first letter only* of each word, or the *first two only*, or the *whole word*. Then even the less quick children will have a sense of completion and can expect credit for their efforts.

Action Sentences

Refer regularly to your Scope and Sequence Chart for action sentences at each STEP level. Vary your presentation: on the board, on an overhead projector, on flashcards. Give children turns at being the presenter so that they can feel the power of words as their classmates silently read and then spring into action.

Develop More Displays

Collect **t** words to build a tower for Ticking Tom. Collect **f** words to build a fire station – one word on every other brick. Collect **m** words to place in the jaws of a huge head of Munching Mike, and so on.

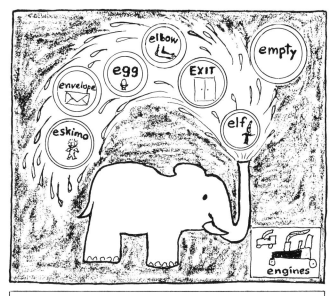

Eddy Elephant is spraying 'e' words.

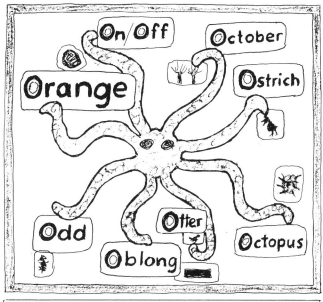

This octopus has lots of 'o' words.

Lamp Lady

Present Lamp Lady Lucy as helpful and protective. She lights up Letterland with her lovely lemon-coloured light. She makes sure no one gets lost. She lives in a lighthouse on Land's End (an L-shaped peninsula) in Letterland.

Like Mr A from Asia, the Lamp Lady has come from a far away place to live in Letterland. You and the children can decide from exactly where. (Pick up any suitable ethnic theme.)

Ⓟ Flashcards

Lamp Lady's Shape

There is *one* striking thing about Lamp Lady's looks. She looks just like the number *one*! She is tall, long and thin, like number one, and as straight as straight can be.

If you are wondering *why* she looks just like number one, the people of Letterland sometimes wonder, too. They have thought of only *one* possible reason. Maybe, it is because she is a neat and tidy lady who always likes doing things carefully, *one by one*. Can anyone here think of any other reason why Lamp Lady looks like the number one?

Allow discussion. There is no need to find a specific reason. It is good to keep some questions open.

Lamp Lady's Sound

Lamp Lady Lucy **loves** singing softly to herself. You can tell that her favourite songs must be **lullabies**, because whenever she goes into a word, it sounds as though she is starting to sing one. '**Lll.., lll.., lll.., lll..**', she sings.

So now that you have met Lamp Lady Lucy, look out for her in words and **listen** for her sound. Can you hear her at the beginning of her name, **L**amp **L**ady **L**ucy?

Write Lamp Lady's Letter

 Air Trace

 Handwriting Verse

 Listen and Write

 Involve Parents

 Play-Act

 Sing Song

 Action Sentences

Capital L

For Capital **L** the Lamp Lady takes a deep breath and gets bigger. In her case, however, her **legs** also grow **longer** – so **long** in fact, that she has to sit down with her **legs on the line**.

ll: Two Lamp Ladies

Many useful little words end in double **l**. (e.g. **bell, doll, fill, fell, hill, tell, will, well**, etc) Why should these **little** words be spelt with two **ll**'s instead of one? The Letterland reason is as follows.

In most **long** words, Lamp Lady Lucy feels happy because she **likes** being in a crowd. But if she finds herself in any **little** words with only one or two other letters for company, she feels a **little bit lonely**. So what does she do? She calls in her best friend, Lamp Lady Linda, to join her. This pleases everybody because together they really **light up little** words.

Code Sheet 17: l, L and ll

Oral lemon coloured light   lick a lolly   long, longer
         lemon/yellow/lime   like a lolly   longest legs

Picture Coding   Overwrite hollow **l**'s and **L**'s in thick yellow. Draw coding details in yellow or orange.

Revision   Re-read some or all of Sheets 1 – 2, 6 – 12 and 14 – 16 (**c, a, d, t, s, i, n, y, g, o, p, k** and **e**). Overwrite **l**'s in yellow but only add the picture coding to a few as there are over 30 **l**'s awaiting discovery!

Suggestion   A 'Lamp Lady List' with sections for Lamp Lady on her own, and with Lamp Lady Linda.

First Dictionary

Award **l** sticker. Place it on page 12. Add any of the words beginning with **l** listed on the 3-D section of the Scope and Sequence Charts. Enter more **m** words as well.

Note. Lamp Lady can get lonely in long words too. (e.g. **yellow**). Note that words **all, tall, ball** etc are best treated as sight words at this stage. Code them with boxes as necessary, because they contain irregular vowels. (See the Main Pack for the Letterland explanation for -all/-al and -full/-ful.)

113

Vase of Violets

The letter **v** is a relatively simple one to teach. It has a simple shape and is one of the very few letters that never changes it sound.

Explain that this letter is a vase of violets, lovely violets with velvet petals and velvet leaves. These violets grow in the valleys of Letterland where children make special vases for them. They use these vases of violets to decorate words like **have** and **give** and **live**.

Ⓟ Flashcards

Vase of Violets: Shape and Sound

Help the children to discover the sound of the letter from the beginning of its name: Vvvase of Vvvviolets.

Help them count the five leaves and petals on each violet and to listen to the **v** sound each time they say number *five*.

five...

Capital V

Why do some vases look bigger? Because Letterland children bring them nearer to us to show us that a word is important.

Write the Vase of Violets' Letter

Air Trace

Finger Trace

Handwriting Verse

Listen and Write

Involve Parents

Play-Act

Sing

The **e** in the **-ve** ending is neither Eddy Elephant nor Mr E. So what is the reason for the silent **e** at the ends of words like **have** and **live** and **give**?

Well, in Letterland there is a reason for most things. This **e** is a Silent Vase-Prop **e**. It makes no sound at all. But it does have a special job – to stop a Vase of Violets from blowing over at the end of a word. *Inside* words these vases are protected from the Letterland winds. Because these winds can be very strong – and of course they always blow in the Reading Direction – these **very valuable vases** of **violets all need propping up.**

To write the vase-prop **e**, the children can simply join up **v** and **e** as for cursive writing. If they want to show that it is a silent letter they write it in dots.

The ve Picture Code Card is in the Main Pack. Meanwhile use the grey silent **e** Picture Code Card when building words such as **have, give,** with the Cards.

3-D Words: have, give, live

To help with spelling **have, give** and **live** follow up your explanation with some miming.

Appoint a Vase-Prop **e** child to wear the grey Silent **e** card. Sequence three children as **h-a-v**. Then call upon a group to come and stand to the left of **hav**. Have everyone blow hard in the Reading Direction. The Vase of Violets child should stagger, as though about to fall to the right. Then the appointed **e** child should rush in and prop up the vase.
Repeat with different children, for **giv-e** and **liv-e**.

Code Sheet 18: v/ve

Oral	wide/narrow	live/keep alive	spill/spilling/spilt
	vase/bowl	five petals/leaves	violet/mauve

Picture Code   Overwrite **v**'s in any dark colour. Add violets. Listen, confirm *no* sound, then add Silent Vase-Prop **e**'s in red. Draw in big violets. Count 5 petals. Add 5 leaves in vase and water.

Revision   Re-read for fluency Code Sheets 11–17 (**g,o,f** and **l**). Compare **of** with **off** on Sheets 12 and 13 (**o** and **f**). Code **v**'s on Sheets 11 and 17 (**g** and **l**). Overwrite grey Vase-Prop **e**'s in red. Revise **l**'s on Sheet 18 (**v**).

First Dictionary

Award **v** sticker. Place on page 22. The word **velvet** can be added, and after STEP 24: **rR**, the much more useful word **very**.

Costume Box

Make Vase of Violets headdresses.

Wicked Water Witch

Now comes a 'baddie' character, the Wicked Water Witch! She is a real trouble-maker for any child who wants to learn how to read and spell well. This is not mere fiction! The presence of **w** in words accounts for many shifts in vowel sounds, both predictable (e.g. **aw, ow, ew**) and less predictable (e.g. one-off words such as **was, want, woman, world**).

Use this witch as a catalyst by presenting her as a character for the children to outwit. How? By learning all her wicked ways in words!

Ⓟ Flashcards

(For teachers opting for the gentler Winnie, the Water-sprite pictogram instead of the Witch, picture code the Water-sprite in blue. For **wh**, page 118, add a wand instead of broomstick to illustrate her **wh**isking away the Hat Man's hat.)

The Wicked Witch's Letter Shape

Before you start, write six capital **M**'s and six capital **W**'s on the board, making the letters thick.

Also find time to discuss what **windmills** are.

Introduce the Witch on both sides of the Picture Code Card. Liken the middle of her letter to a very small island with two pools on either side. These are the witch's very own swimming pools. They also hold all the water she needs for her wicked spelling spells.

First, have six children come and add water to the **w**'s on the board, in blue if possible. Then have them draw the Witch perched on her island in the middle.

Discuss the similarities and differences between Munching Mike's Mum's shape and the Witch's letter which holds water. (Let them picture code Munching Mike's Mum to reinforce the differences.)

The Witch's Sound

Discuss where in Letterland the Wicked Water Witch might live. North? South? East? Or **Www**est? (Elicit 'west'.)

Why yes! How ever did you know? And what do you think the **wwweather** might be like where she lives in the **Wwwest**? Dry and sunny? Or **wwwet** and **wwwindy**?

By now the children should be sensitive to alliteration. So, hopefully, they will be able to answer this question correctly even before you formally teach the **w** sound. If not, help them to match up the initial **w** sounds in her name with the initial **w** sounds in **wet** and **windy**.

Yes, the weather where the Wicked Water Witch lives is **wild** and **wet** and **windy**. It rains and rains, and the **west wind whines** through the trees day and night. The **wind** makes a sound like this: **wwww...wwwww...wwww**. Perhaps that is **why** the Wicked Water Witch makes a sound just like the **wind** whenever she turns up in a **word**!

Write the Wicked Witch's Letter

Air Trace

Finger Trace

Handwriting Verse

Listen and Write

Involve Parents

Play Act

Sing

3-D Words: wind, mill, windmill

Call four children up to create and discover that they have made the word **wind**. Meanwhile ask a fifth child to quickly draw an **i** on a stiff card and code it with an ink bottle, to serve as an extra **i** card.

Create **mill** with this child, a Munching Mike and two children holding the double-**l** card between them. Then have the eight children move together to form the word **windmill**, and help them to discover what bigger word the two smaller words have produced.

Disband them. Appoint eight other children to make **windmill** again. This time the rest of the group must guide them into the right sequence by saying the word *windmill* in 'slow-speak'.

Explore the other words on the Scope and Sequence Charts, on Picture Code Cards and on the board. Suggest spelling pictures. (If children want to include **wet witch** among these spelling pictures, have them picture code **witch** as shown and promise stories about Tom, Clever Cat and the Hat Man later.)

Code Sheet 19: wW

Oral

| windmill -wwww | well (for water) | spill/spilling |
| wind/water -wwww | well, well, well | spilt |

Picture Code Overwrite broken-line **w**'s in dark blue. Draw witch in black or blue or just add a witch's hat over each **w**. Water: *light* blue. Ring *yes*. Discuss who spilt water (open ended). Accept all 'could be' answers.

Revision Code **e**'s on **W** Sheet. Re-read *any* code sheets you think useful for practising fluency. (There are no **w**'s before Sheet 19.)

First Dictionary

Award **w** sticker. Place it on page 23. The words **wet**, **well** and **will** can be added, and **went west**. Ideally all **wh** words (see below) should be written on the right after the children have been given Code Sheet 34: **wh**.

Proof that the Witch is Wicked

Proof that the Witch is wicked is right to hand in many words, and especially in five of the 100 most used words in the language: **when, what, where, which** and **why**. For simplicity's sake, at first just use the word **when** as an example.

Code one side of your **when** flashcard with the Wicked Water Witch whacking off the Hat Man's Hat. On the reverse, write the **h** in dots to indicate a silent letter. On the board write *when* very large using the side of a piece of chalk.

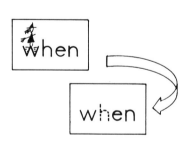

When the Wicked Water Witch goes into a word she needs to be able to see ahead in the Reading Direction, just as everyone else does in Letterland. So just imagine how she feels when she finds a *tall* letter right next to her. Who is he? (Add his head and feet.) On top of that he's wearing a *hat* (add his hat). That makes it even harder for her to see ahead in the Reading Direction!

So she takes her broomstick and **whacks** the Hat Man's hat off!

The poor Hairy Hat Man is so startled that he can't speak. That is **why when** you want to read this word you will get it wrong if you try to sound it out like this: www-**hhh**ĕn.

118

Instead, you have to remember that the Hairy Hat Man makes no sound at all in this word. And whose fault is that?

Elicit 'the Wicked Witch'!

Warn the children that not only does the Witch whack the Hat Man's hat off in this word (and several others, too) to show the Hat Man how much she hates him being in her way. She also likes making *reading* and *spelling* difficult for *anyone* who is just learning how. She thinks that if she upsets the Hat Man so he can't say '**hhh**' she might make it harder for people to read this word.

So how do we say **when**?

Elicit 'when'.

Yes, it is **when**. The Wicked Witch also thinks that because you can't hear the Hat Man making his usual whispery '**hhh**' sound in the word **when** you might forget to write his letter down **when** you go to spell **when**. Then she would be glad.

So are you going to let the Wicked Witch trick you in the word **when**? (Elicit 'No'!) Well, we will hope not. But don't be too surprised if she does catch you out sometimes, at first, until you get used to her wicked ways.

Bring **when** into the growing number of words in your sentence work. (See your Scope and Sequence Charts.) It will make combinations like the following possible:

The Wicked Water Witch is wicked in **when**.
I can clap **when** I am sitting.
I can yell **when** I am kicking.

When I am ⎰ sad
⎱ glad I like to   (discussion)
     hot

I am glad **when** I can ⎰ kick
⎱ lick ice cream
   yell
   have milk
   give Hairy Hat Man his hat

Action Sentences

The word **when** will also add vim and vigour to your action sentences, e.g. wink when I clap, clap when I wink, etc since now the children's responses are time-linked. Think of other action sentences besides those listed on the Scope and Sequence Chart.

You can also turn the action sentences into a game for two or more children to play together, by writing selected ones on to sentence cards which they can hold up for each other to silently read, then act out.

The Question Words

The Witch and the Hat Man have only one thing in common. They both love to ask questions. That is why you always see them both in these five words: **when? which? why? what?** and **where?**

Sing about them (see Letterland Audio Tape No. 1 and accompanying Songbook) to help make these high-usage words very familiar and therefore easier to spell. Teach the final verse for **who?** at a later date.

Make spelling pictures of them based on Code Sheet 34: **wh**. The bigger the better!

Code Sheet 34: wh

Picture Coding   Listen and confirm which hollow letter is silent. Colour in **w** in dark blue and **h** in grey, although Hat Man's hat remains green and face can be coloured pink.

Discuss how Annie Apple is clearly so startled in **what** that no one can expect her to say **ă**, as usual. (One more difficult spelling to blame on the Wicked Witch!)

More Proof that the Witch is Wicked

The proof, this time, is in numbers. Why do we hear the Witch's sound coming from the **o** in the word **one**? For one answer see Letterland Audio Tape No. 1 and Songbook.

For more about numbers see page 141 and Code Sheet 36.

Reminder   Now is a good time to learn the **sw** and **tw** 'Consonant Caper' songs.

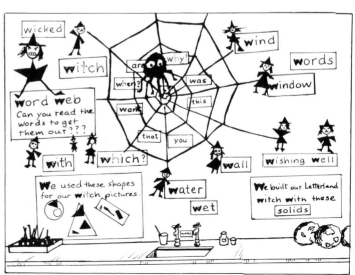

Jumping Jim

The letter **j** is almost unique in the English alphabet because it never changes its sound or becomes a silent letter. So introduce Jumping Jim as a good, reliable fellow. You can always count on him.

Like many athletes in the modern Olympics, Jumping Jim is also a champion. So you can present him as a hero – the all-time high jumping champion of Letterland! Not only can he jump sky-high (witness the capital letter shape) but he can even juggle while he jumps!

Ⓟ Flashcards

Jumping Jim's Shape

Jumping Jim always **jumps** in the Reading Direction in words, so of course the curve of his letter shape must show his knees bending round to his **jogging shoes** behind him.

Jumping Jim **juggles** with balls, so fast that you can never see more than *one* ball at a time (the **j**-dot). Just think how difficult it must be to **juggle while you jump**. It is almost impossible! No wonder Jumping Jim wins all the jumping competitions held in Letterland every **January, June** and **July**.

Let the children try jumping and juggling around the playground (in the Reading Direction ideally) during playtime. They will soon see for themselves how impossible it is to do *both* at once, and really admire Jumping Jim for knowing how.

Jumping Jim's Sound

Discover Jumping Jim's sound by *beginning* to say his name: **j..., j..., j...** Discourage 'juh'. **J** is a low frequency letter because so many words are spelt with soft **g** instead. So present Jumping Jim as a somewhat modest champion, a useful characterisation later on when your children must choose as quickly as possible, whether to spell a word with **j** or **g**. The odds are very much in favour of **g**.

Write the Jumping Jim's Letter

Air
Trace

Handwriting
Verse

Listen
and Write

Involve
Parents

Play
Act

Sing

Capital J

Capital **J** will not be needed very often because words beginning with it are also few and far between. Names, however, are a different matter. Because these are all-important words, Jumping Jim likes nothing better than to start a child's name with a sky high jump! (e.g. Josephine, John, Jack, Jane, etc.)

So, lots of children can enjoy picture coding him up in the clouds at the start of their name. If you have any children with foreign names starting with **J** sounding like **Y**, help them to decide on a reason themselves: e.g. "Jim must be juggling yellow yo-yos up there in the clouds – just for a change!"

Code Sheet 20: jJ

Oral
| jump/leap | jam (fruit) | jelly (juice) |
| juggle/enjoy | in a jam | just juice |

Picture Code   Listen and overwrite **j**'s in brown. Draw in **J** clouds. Discuss relative positions of **j** and **J**. Code Jim in red or orange for contrast.

Revision   There are no **j**'s before Sheet 20. Revise **n** and **o** on this Sheet by comparing and coding Nick, Mr O and Oscar Orange in **no** and **on**.

Reading at Home: Code Sheets 12–20

This may be a good time to send the children home with some or all of Sheets 12–20 to read to their parents.

Ideally, they should be confident enough by now to read them well even if their parents cover up the illustrations.

First Dictionary

Award **j** sticker. Place it on page 10. The words **jam, jet** and **jacket** can be added now. Wait until after Step 22: **uU** and then add **jump**.

Reinforce the ing ending

Jump**ing** Jim's name provides a good opportunity to revise the **ng** story. (Have the children *tell you* the story.) Then search through all the character names covered so far to find which other ones contain **-ing**. (They are: Munching Mike, Ticking Tom, Kicking King, and now Jumping Jim.)

Revise other words ending in **-ing** on your Scope and Sequence Charts.

Let the children discover for themselves more verbs with **-ing** and realise the satisfaction of now being able to sound out many of them by themselves.

If you did not introduce Code Sheet 33: **ing** at the end of STEP 15: **kK** and **ng**, you may wish to now.

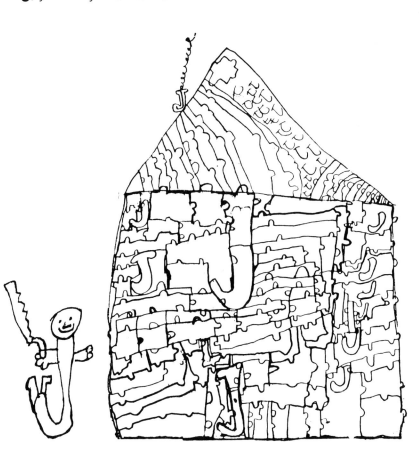

6-year old Jamie's jigsaw house, Gamlingay Primary School, Cambs.

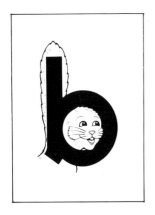

Bouncy Ben

Another very lively letter comes next – Bouncy Ben. Bouncy Ben is a bright-eyed, brown bunny, who bounces along in words saying '**b... b... b...**' as he bounces.

Doubtless you will have had to tell curious children 'who' the character is between Annie Apple and Clever Cat on the frieze long before now. The delay in focusing on him, however, is deliberate. It is one more precaution against **b/d** confusions.

To make the differences between **d** and **b** completely clear *at all times* take care always to use the pronouns, she/her/hers for Dippy Duck and he/him/his for Bouncy Ben. (For children who arrive in your class already confusing **b** and **d**, further support is available in the Main Pack.) Introduce your second **b** (Bouncy Barbara) later for words with **bb**.

Ⓟ Flashcards

Bouncy Ben's Shape and Sound

Stress the importance of Bouncy Ben's **big brown** ears which stick up so straight as he **bounces** along in the Reading Direction. Compare them with Poor Peter's ears which droop. Far from feeling unhappy about *his* ears, Bouncy Ben often **boasts** about them, because they are so **big** and **brown** and **beautiful**!

Bouncy Ben has six **brothers**! He lives in a **burrow**! His burrow is ... (let the children decide) ... **by a bridge**? At the **back of a barn**? In the **blackberry bushes**? etc.

His sound (as with all other Letterland characters) is reliably at the **beginning** of his name. Make sure the children avoid saying 'buh' by clipping their voices as much as possible after sending a burst of air through their lips.

Barbara

Bouncy Ben has 6 baby brothers.

Air Trace

Handwriting Verse

Listen and Write

Involve Parents

Play Act

Sing

124

3-D Words: big, beg, bag, bags

There are many more words which the children can now make in 3-D with the Picture Code Cards and learn to write from your slow-speak dictation. Choose those you prefer from the Scope and Sequence Chart.

Capital B

Explain capital **B** as a picture of Bouncy Ben doing his **balancing** trick:

To begin important words, Bouncy Ben always balances his **bright blue ball** in **between** his **beautiful, big brown** ears. He bets you can't do that!

Be Bouncy Ben

Most youngsters will enjoy showing you that in fact they *can* balance a ball between their ears (using arms), just like Bouncy Ben. They may even balance one *while bouncing*!

You may like to reinforce Bouncy Ben's sound further by playing one of Bouncy Ben's favourite games:
    'bat the balloon' (a blue one, ideally)
    'throw the bean bag in the basket'
    'blowing bubbles'
Let these words lead to interesting artwork.

Code Sheet 21: bB

Oral	bend	break	big/biggest	bounce	both
	bent	broken	best, boast	balance	

Picture Code   Overwrite **b**'s in dark blue. Code both Ben and ball light blue, (brown can obscure letter shape). Add missing **b**'s. Overwrite and code **d**'s in orange for contrast. Colour Ben's bed blanket in blue. Either have the children box **ou** and soft **c**'s in **Bouncy** and **bouncing** or ignore at this stage.

Revision   Find, listen, and code **b** on Code Sheets 10 and 18. (All other words with **b** occur in sheets still to come.)

First Dictionary

Award **b** sticker. Place it on page 2. Add any words from the 3-D section of the Scope and Sequence Chart. Enter more words on the **c** page, too.

Mural: a,b,c,d

If you still have your first mural on display the children may like now to add Bouncy Ben and his brothers in the background.

Costume Box

Now is a good time to picture code the **B** in Clever Cat's Costume Box by adding Bouncy Ben's face and ball. Add play-acting props in the form of ears or masks for Bouncy Ben and his brothers, which the children can make in a crafts period.

Denise Lambert's class, Alton Primary School, Hants.

Bouncy Ben Working Display

Place this mural on the left side of the wall which already shows Dippy Duck and her Duck Door on the right.

Show Bouncy Ben in his **burrow**. If possible, construct it so that the children can bounce Bouncy Ben out of his burrow and **back** in again. Discuss how, when he bounces out, they can see the rest of his **body**.

Discuss how, like Dippy Duck, Bouncy Ben never turns away from the Reading Direction, even to **bounce back** into his burrow.

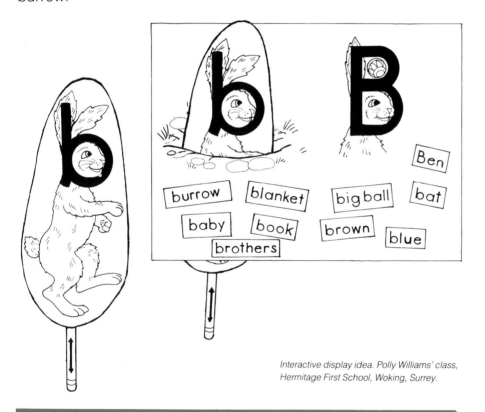

burrow blanket big ball Ben

baby book brown bat

brothers blue

Interactive display idea. Polly Williams' class, Hermitage First School, Woking, Surrey.

Quick Dash

Your daily dash will now include **b,d** and **p**. Make sure the children recognise these letters *without* the support of the Pictograms before you introduce **qu** in STEP 23.

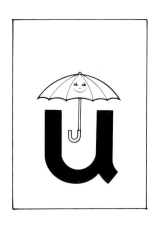

Uppy Umbrella
& Mr U

As you introduce the last of the five vowels you will again be emphasising the short vowel sound first. You will be casually introducing the Vowel Man, Mr U, too, but you will not introduce words to read or to spell containing long **u** until your children are very sure of the short vowel sound.

Bring a real umbrella to school with you to start this STEP.

Ⓟ Flashcards

Uppy Umbrella's Letter Shape

Open and shut your umbrella. Discuss weather in general.

Sometimes in Letterland it can be *very* rainy, indeed.
People find that one minute it is sunny; the next minute, the rain is pouring down! That's why you are lucky if you have an umbrella to stand **under**. Put **up** your umbrella and you will stay just as dry as if the sun were still shining.

All the umbrellas in Letterland are very **understanding**. They are very glad to let anyone stand **under** them who doesn't want to get wet.

Hold up the plain side of your Picture Code Card.

The sudden rainstorms in Letterland mean that this letter has to be looked after very carefully, because it is shaped rather like a tub. People call it 'the umbrella-letter' because it always needs an umbrella above it to keep it from filling up with water when it rains. The important job of keeping this letter dry goes to Uppy Umbrella. Would you like to see what Uppy Umbrella looks like?

Show Pictogram side of card.

Uppy Umbrella's Sound

Here she is. She is a happy-go-lucky little umbrella who loves getting wet! But she never lets her umbrella-letter get wet. Oh no! She keeps it **covered up**, not only on rainy days but on sunny days, too. Think how dreadful it would be if the Wicked Water Witch were to **fill it up** with water to use for some of her wicked spelling spells!

When you see Uppy Umbrella's letter you will usually hear Uppy Umbrella saying '**u...**' as she carefully covers up the letter.

Have the children stand up and form protective umbrella shapes with their arms to mime Uppy Umbrella as they say, '**ŭ..., ŭ...,ŭ..., ŭ...**'.

Write Uppy Umbrella's Letter

Air Trace

Finger Trace

Handwriting Verse

Listen and Write

Involve Parents

Play Act

Sing

3-D Words: up, us, fun, sun, luck

The children should by now be able to write down many 3-D Words listed on your Scope and Sequence Chart without necessarily having to make them in 3-D first, or form them on the Picture Code Cards. They should be getting quite practised in taking down any of the words on this list marked as good slow-speak words.

Mr U, the Uniform Man

Hold up your Mr U card, Pictogram side showing.

You can tell that umbrellas must be important in Letterland because an important looking man called Mr U, the Uniform Man, has the job of looking after them all. We know *he* must be important. Otherwise, he wouldn't be wearing a uniform!

For more about Mr U, see below. Meanwhile concentrate on the short sound made by Uppy Umbrella.

Code Sheet 22: uU

Oral   up/upside down   shut it   undo/do up   cover up
          under/sun/umbrella fold it up   open up   uncover

Picture Code   Overwrite **u** and **U** in turquoise or blue. Use any bright colour for umbrellas.

Revision   Code Mr O in **going** on **u** sheet. Then re-read Code Sheets 3,14 and 20 (**d, p** and **j**). Discover, listen and code **u**'s.

First Dictionary

Award **u** sticker. Place it on page 21. The word **up** can be added now, and **under** after STEP 24: **rR**. Enter more words on the **t** page, too.

Spelling Pictures

Code Sheet 31: Mr U

This Code Sheet lists the two most useful words beginning with long **u**. The only others within the 3,000 most used words are:

using	usual	uniform	unit
used	usually	union	unite

You can therefore stress that it is very **un**usual to see Mr U at the beginning of words. Instead, emphasise how he often appears at the *end* of one little word, **you**, because the Yo-yo Man has a nice big yo-yo to give him there. This will save some of the bewilderment children otherwise feel when they try to spell the word **you** starting with **u** and then cannot imagine what letter comes next!

Spelling Picture: you

Have each child make one! They can also add the Yo-yo Man and turn the **o** into a yo-yo in the word **you** as shown on Code Sheet 31 if they wish. Then they will have it as a permanent mnemonic in their Letterland folders.

Quarrelsome Queen & her Quiet Room

The words available beginning with **qu** determine the temperament of Letterland's queen. She is beautiful of course, as all queens traditionally seem to be, but she is also **quick** to **quarrel.** This is why everyone calls her 'the Quarrelsome Queen'.

The characterisation of the queen can provide fruitful discussion material. Children know at first hand, alas, about cross adults. A chance to discuss with you anyone they know who gets cross as **quickly** as Letterland's queen can give them an opening to talk.

Ⓟ Flashcards

| queen | Be quick | Quarrelsome Queen | The question is |

The Quarrelsome Queen's Shape

The queen quarrels with the king and everyone else in Letterland. Normally, she has no less than *nine* quarrels a day which may explain why her letter looks like a nine.

She is also proud of her splendid long hair. This is why she insists on taking her royal umbrella with her wherever she goes. Just think! Supposing it suddenly rained on her beautiful hair! The very thought makes her feel **quite queer**! She is certain to **quarrel** with anyone who tries to stop her from keeping her umbrella right beside her in words!

Further proof as to how **quarrelsome** this queen can be lies in the fact that she refuses to face in the Reading Direction in words. She will certainly quarrel with anyone who tries to turn her around!

The Quarrelsome Queen's Sound

The queen's sound, as with all of the letters, will be on the children's lips the moment they *start* to say her name. The **qu** sound is difficult, however, because it is really *two* letters' sounds said rapidly together: **cw**.

9 quarrelling queens

by Michael Johnson

In the event, by making this sound herself the queen saves Clever Cat from ever having to be next to the Wicked Witch in a word!

130

Write the Queen's' Letter

 Air Trace

 Finger Trace

 Handwriting Verse

 Listen and Write

 Involve Parents

 Play Act

 Sing

Capital Q

The capital **Q** shape is the Quarrelsome Queen's Quiet Room where she goes to recover from all her quarrelling. Help the children to notice how she won't even go into the Quiet Room, without keeping her precious umbrella within reach, (i.e. never write either small **q** or capital **Q** without adding **u**. (Exceptions are always foreign, not English words.)

Quick Dash

Tell the children you want the 'Quick Dash' to be extra **quick**, now that the queen's card is going to be in it. But they must *not* reply when you hold up the single **q** card – only when you hold up the **qu** card. This way you emphasise the fact that the queen won't even *speak* unless given her umbrella.

3-D Words: queen, see, keep, sleep

Write the word **queen** on the board first. Then appoint a queen, an umbrella child, two Mr E's and a Naughty Nick.

(Remind the children that Eddy Elephant never turns up in a word with another elephant right beside him – elephants are too big to share one sound! Instead, two **e**'s side-by-side will always be Mr E and his twin brother, both saying their name '**ē**' loud and clear.)

Place the two Mr E's and Naughty Nick on the left of the class. Put the queen and umbrella child on the class's right.

First, get the queen to pull the umbrella child to the centre of the room, crossly muttering '**qu.., qu.., qu...**' as they both move *against* the Reading Direction. Next, the two Mr E's should walk correctly in the Reading Direction, the first Mr E saying his name '**ē**' as they come. Then Naughty Nick should set off from the left saying '**nnnnnn**' until he is in position for you to orchestrate all five children to pronounce the three sounds in sequence: **queen**!

Go on to make **see, keep** and **sleep**.

131

Code Sheet 23: qu/Qu

Oral Quarrelsome/cross   queen's quilt   questions
            quiet/quietly   liquid/juice? stains? quick/quickly

Revision Re-read Code Sheets 12 – 23, looking especially
for question marks. (They are printed in grey because they are
silent symbols.)

First Dictionary

Award **q** sticker. Place on page 17. Have the children **quickly**
add **u**'s! Now **queen** and **quick** can be added.

Spelling Pictures

Make spelling pictures of the **queen**, and of a **queen bee**.

Qu Display

Ask the children to collect words with **qu** in them. Ask them to check
to see for themselves, in every case, whether it is really true that the
queen never appears in a word without her umbrella. (See
page 15 for an example of a **qu** display.)

Robber Red

The vitality of Letterland stems in part from the many parallels to real life. The figure of Robber Red produces yet another of these parallels. In real life there are people who break rules and laws. Every child will know at least a little about what it means to take something which does not belong to them or to have something taken from them. "Mine!" is an early word in most children's vocabulary, used both offensively and defensively, which may explain why they are invariably intrigued by Letterland's chief law-breaker, Robber Red. He taps the excitement inherent in the reality of right and wrong. As a result, once you have alerted them to his shape and sound, they love to 'catch' him in words.

Robber Red is the ringleader of a gang of trouble-makers. He is a real rascal, but he always makes the same growling sound at the beginning of words, and also just inside them (**br, cr, dr, fr, gr, pr, tr, thr, scr, str** and **wr**).

Ⓟ Flashcards

Robber Red's Shape and Sound

Hold up the plain side of your **r** Picture Code Card.

The Wicked Water Witch is not the *only* trouble maker in Letterland. This card shows you the letter shape of a man called Robber Red. Robber Red always **runs** in the **Reading** Direction growling '**rrr**' as he **runs**.

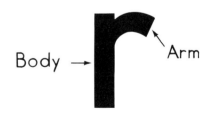

Encourage the children to imagine the upright line as the robber's body and the rightward line as Robber Red's outstretched arm. Discuss where his head and legs must be. Before turning to the Pictogram side, discuss colour.

What colour do you think Robber Red's clothes will be?

They will know that the answer is **red** from the alphabet frieze. However, the sound of **r** is difficult to pronounce in isolation because it distorts so easily to 'ruh' or 'er'. So take every opportunity to emphasise his sound accurately in running speech. The word **red** gives you repeated opportunities.

133

Yes, **rrred**. All his clothes are rrred. His cap is rrred. His trousers are red. His socks are red. His boots are red. Even his hair is red, not just a carrot colour but **rrreally rrred**, just as rrred as his *red* clothes! So now you know why everyone in Letterland calls this bad man Robber **Red**. What direction will Robber Red be **running** in.

Elicit 'the Rrrreading Direction!'

What sort of things does Rrrobber Rrred rrun off with? (Only things beginning with his sound!) Let the children think of some things he might take.

Write Robber Red's Letter

Air Trace   Handwriting Verse   Listen and Write   Involve Parents   Play Act   Sing

Capital R

When Robber Red takes a deep breath to start an important word he certainly gets bigger! He also looks fatter! Why the big bulge in front? Because he has just stuffed some stolen goods inside his sweater to hide them from us! He also hopes that by changing his shape he will make it more difficult for you to **rrrrecognise** him!

Today is the day to picture code the initial **R** on all your Reading Direction signs.

But it's not Robber Red!

Of the 250 most-used words in the English language, 58 contain an **r**. Yet the children will only be able to hear Robber Red growling in 18 of them, listed below (highest usage ones listed first).

1) from	**2)** every	red	three	**3)** children	street
right	green	room	tree	rabbit	train
	ran	round	very	road	
	read	run			

Therefore, as soon as you venture into any reading material outside this Starter Pack, the children will encounter many, many exceptions.

Given Robber Red and his gang, however, you will not have to apologise for these exceptions. Simply blame them on Robber Red's gang instead. Like the Wicked Water Witch, Robber Red likes to make learning to read as hard as he can! This is why he has a robber gang.

At this stage encourage the children as a first strategy to learn irregular words like **are, her, or, our, your, bird,** and **year,** etc. as whole word shapes. Use boxes to ensure that they do not waste time trying to sound out these words. Promise some stories to explain them later. (All these are covered in the Main Pack.)

Code Sheet 24: rR

Oral rob/take/grab rascal/grrrowl rip/trip ring on a finger
rule-breaker run/rush/race red ruby ring around a word

First Dictionary

Award **r** sticker. Place on page 18. Now **red, run** and **ran** can all be added, plus other Scope and Sequence Chart words. Enter more words on **s** page, too.

Spelling Pictures

Consonant Capers

Reminder Now is a good time to learn any of these Consonant Capers' songs: **br, cr, dr, fr, gr, pr, str, shr.**

(Alternative **r** pictogram, Red Racer, the Roller Skater.)

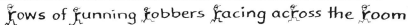
Rows of running robbers racing across the room

Magdalen Gates 1st School, Norwich

135

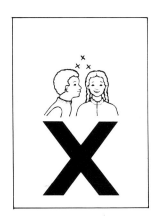

Kissing Cousins

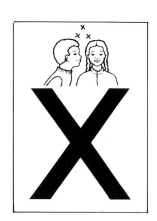

Describe **x** as a 'very loving letter' because when it stands on its own it means 'kiss'. Show the card's plain side first. Discuss the shape as being like two crossed sticks. On the Pictogram side introduce Letterland's kissing cousins, Max and Maxine.

Flashcards

Max and Maxine   next   box

The Shape and Sound of x

Explain that the 'real' reason Max and Maxine kiss above their letter is to remind us of their letter's sound in words. It is 'k-ss', (the word 'kiss' said in a whisper so that we do not hear the vowel.) Have everyone *whisper* 'kiss', listening to themselves all the while, paying special attention to their own throat and tongue movements.

Explain that they won't spot Max and Maxine kissing very often in words (there are only *two* in the 250 most used English words: **next** and **box**), but to keep a sharp look-out for them all the same.

Have the children listen together for the **x** sound in sentences such as: Can Ma**x** fi**x** the bo**x**?

It is helpful if they *whisper* the whole sentence to make the 'k-ss' sound easier to notice.

Write Max and Maxine's Letter

Air
Trace

Handwriting
Verse

Listen
and Write

Involve
Parents

Play
Act

Sing

Spelling: x? or -cks?

When it comes to spelling the 'k-ss' sound, one reason the kissing cousins are seldom seen is because the job is often done by three other letters instead.

Leave the children to guess 'who' these three may be. (It should emerge on Code Sheet 25: **xX** in the word **socks**.)

Congratulate the first children to make this discovery. In spelling, they will need to use **-cks** the most. You may like to start two lists: for **-x** and **-cks**, to discover gradually exactly how few words appear in the **-x** list compared with the **-cks** list.

Note. The children may also discover words ending in **-ks** (looks, weeks) and **-kes** (makes, likes). Again, congratulate them and help them to start a third, and a fourth list.

fox	fix
box	
wax	

socks	ticks
blocks	picks
bricks	packs
kicks	pecks
rocks	
tricks	
necks	
backs	

X-Rays and Xylophones

Pictures of x-rays or of xylophones on alphabet friezes are not pedagogically sound for the introductory stages of alphabet teaching. They are entirely misleading since in each case they only apply to two words ('exs' in **X-ray** and **X-mas** or 'zzz' in **xylophone** and **xerox**). Both ignore the 'kss' sound in many more useful words, e.g. **fix, mix, six, ox, box, fox, wax, next, expect, expense, express, extra,** etc.

3-D Words: six, fix, fox, box, next

See the Scope and Sequence Charts for further words.

Code Sheet 25: xX

Oral	wax (crayons)	six	fix	mix	box
	wax (candles)	sixteen	fixed	mixer	boxes

Picture Coding   Code **x** in red. Compare **cks** sound in **socks**. Overwrite **cks** in thick blue so that all three letters are highlighted as one sound.

Revision   Re-read recent Code Sheets to develop fluency. (There are no **x**'s to discover.)

First Dictionary

Award **x** sticker. Place on page 24 (with **y**.) Explain that Max and Maxine never kiss at the start of a word, so words listed here will begin with other letters. Add **six** and **next** now.

Enter some words on the **y** page now, too.

Exit Signs

Make fresh Exit signs for taking home (as in STEP 16: **eE**). This time the children can picture code all the letters.

Box Games

This game may be used for general revision. Ask each child to bring a little box to school with one little thing in it. Let them place these under the right letters on the frieze, e.g. a box with stamps in it under Sammy Snake. Under **x** place the biggest box with lots of letters in it, written by the children 'with love and xxx' to Max and Maxine.

Use these boxes for memory games, too, e.g. 'Guess what's in Annie Apple's box' and 'What else *could* she have in her box?' etc. Also move the boxes around, for the children to re-sort under the right letters. (This can promote useful discussion, e.g. Why is this box of pins under Dippy Duck's letter? Ah, yes, **d**rawing pins!)

Love and X X X,
from Max
and Maxine

P.S. At the start of 2 or 3 words
I have a quick snooze, like this →
instead of giving Maxine a kiss.

Xylophone   Xerox

Zig Zag Zebra

Zig Zag Zebra tends to be a favourite among quiet and withdrawn children because she is a very shy zebra, rarely showing herself in words. (As already explained, the **z** sound is created far more often by **s** than **z**.) Your second **z** card is Zig Zag's shy friend, Zoe.

Ⓟ Flashcards

Zig Zag Zebra's Shape and Sound

Introduce either side of the Picture Code Card first, but make sure that the children study both sides carefully to notice orientation. Elicit their observation that Zig Zag Zebra is NOT facing in the Reading Direction. Who else does not? (Golden Girl and the Queen).

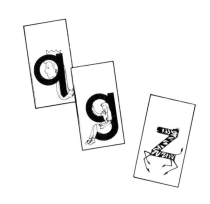

So three letters 'look left' instead of to the right: Golden Girl because she gets giddy, the Queen because she is quarrelsome and Zig Zag Zebra because she is so shy. (Shy people and animals often turn around and face the other way.)

Zig Zag Zebra moves very, very fast. She will **zip** into a word and zip out again so fast that you hardly have time to hear her making a tiny little '**zzz**' sound.

Who else makes a '**zzz**' sound in words? Sammy Snake, of course. Zig Zag Zebra makes exactly the same sound as Sammy Snake when he is sleepy but not because *she* is having a quiet snooze. Far from it. She says '**zzz**' because she is whi**zz**ing along so fast!

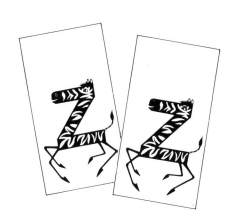

Every once in a blue moon if you are lucky you might see Zig Zag Zebra whizzing along with her best friend Zoe Zebra in a word. Then the sight of not just one but *two* stripy zebras *both* **whizzing** in one word is enough to make anyone quite **dizzy**!

Discuss how fast moving black and white lines can blur to look **fuzzy**. Use these words to make spelling pictures featuring Zig Zag and her shy friend, Zoe Zebra.

Capital Z

Like a number of other letters, to start an important word Zig Zag Zebra just takes a deep breath and gets bigger.

Write Zig Zag Zebra's Letter

Air
Trace

Handwriting
Verse

Listen
and Write

Involve
Parents

Play
Act

Sing

Code Sheet 26: zZ

Oral whiz   zzzoom (comics)   buzz   zig/zag (meanings)
whizzing   zzz (comics)   buzzing   zip along

Picture Coding   Listen, add stripes, etc. to hollow **z**'s.

Revision   Code **ĕ, and ee** on this sheet. There are no **z**'s on earlier sheets because Zig Zag Zebra is so shy!

Complete the Dictionary!

Award **z** sticker. Add **zip, zig zag** and **zebra**. The children's dictionaries will now contain at least 60 words which the children should be able to read and spell without difficulty, on each page, headed by a Letterland friend.

The final page after **z** should be used to collect words in which Vowel Men appear. Take them from the Code Sheets 27 – 31. The same words can be distributed across the dictionary, too, as described below.

From now on the word collecting can concentrate on regular entries which the children will make to consolidate their command of the Scope and Sequence Chart vocabulary, or range much more widely to record their own personal spelling words.

Code Sheets 27-31

If you have not already done so, now is a good time to concentrate on the Code Sheets for Mr A, E, I, O and U (27 – 31). These contain a few key long vowel words which are essential to early reading.

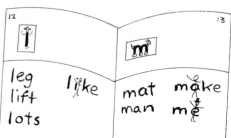

If the children now add them in their freshly-completed dictionaries they should code the long vowel, rather than the initial letter of the word. The stick man then ensures that, when they re-read their list of entries, they do not mispronounce the vowel.

b	– be	n	– no	t	– today
c	– close		nice		the
g	– go		name		these
h	– he	o	– old	u	– use
i	– I, ice		open		useful
k	– kind		only	w	– we
l	– like	p	– play	y	– you
m	– me	s	– say		
	– make		she, so		

Code Sheets 32-35: sh, wh and ng

See Steps 7: sS, 19: wW and 15: kK for details.

Code Sheet 36: 1,2,3,4

This final Code Sheet simply supports spelling. Let each child colour in their own copy. Point out the following.
1. The Witch gets stuck in number **one**. (See Audio Tape No. 1.)
2. Remember 2 pools in the middle of number **two**. Otherwise the wily Witch will have tricked you!
3. There are 3 sounds in number **th-r-ee**.
4. There are 4 letters in number **f-o-u-r**.

Make a Book: a – z

Each child can now design two covers and bind all their Listen and Write Sheets and Code Sheets in them in an **a – z** order. Congratulation time! Award Letterland Passports to all new citizens of Letterland! (See page 160.)

Revision of Steps 1 – 26

The Importance of Vowels

By now the children know the five short vowel sounds and all the consonants. They also have at least a 'nodding acquaintance' with the five Vowel Men as the owners of the apples, elephant, etc.

Now to demonstrate the importance of vowels in words, give out all the consonant Picture Code Cards except **r**, **y** and **w**. Ask the children to make a few words with these 18 cards.

They will soon discover that they cannot even make one! No combination is either pronounceable or meaningful. Why not? Because Annie Apple, Eddy Elephant, Impy Ink, Oscar Orange, Uppy Umbrella and the Vowel Men are all missing. Help the children to deduce how important these five cards and their owners are. Nobody can make a single word without at least one vowel in it!

Convenient general terms from now on for talking about the vowels will be:

Vowel Men for 'long vowels',
Vowel Men's Belongings for 'short vowels'.

You will soon be able to shorten these two phrases to the single word *vowel*, since it has by now acquired meaning in the context of Letterland.

Note. A few words may seem to contain no vowel because **y** is 'doing a job' for a vowel as in **try** or **why**. (These other 'jobs' of the Yo-yo Man are fully explained in the Main Pack.)

A – Z Assembly

There are many ways of achieving valuable revision in Letterland assemblies. (More ambitious ideas are set out in the Main Pack.)

1. Each child can simply walk on dressed as a Letterland character, hold up a letter and say "I am (Annie Apple). What do I say in words?" The whole school replies with the letter's sound.
2. Each child wears a letter and holds up three or four words, written large, on separate pieces of card. For example, "I am (Bouncy Ben). I start all these words." (Use sight words, such as **book, boat, ball,** or regular words, e.g. **big, bag, bug**.) The whole school reads the list as the child points to the words.

3. Perform 3-D word making to music; simply have the children group and re-group rapidly to make short and long words,

e.g. **sun, set, sunset.**

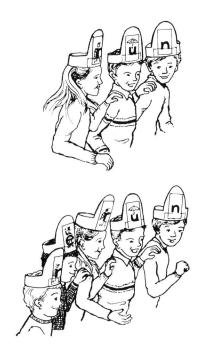

Note: All Letterland characters should enter from the audience's left except **g, qu** and **z**, which should approach the centre from the right.

4. Music and movement miming. The audience guesses what letter is being mimed.

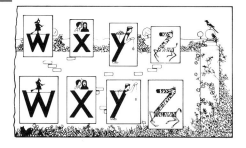

A – Z Frieze Games

Develop the racing game described on page 65, matching Picture Code Cards to frieze letters. Using the full **A – Z,** this matching game becomes more exciting. It also provides good preparation for dictionary work. A child who has run to the *middle* of the frieze to match Munching Mike and nearly to the far *end* for the Witch will soon remember where to look in a dictionary for **m** and **w**.

Kim's Game, Life Scale

This game provides lots of opportunity for repetition of each character name and of its sound.

1. Each child paints and codes a letter on an A4-size stiff card. They all stand on them, placed face down on the floor. They step off, move round the room, return and try to stand on their own card. At a signal from you, they should all pick up the cards to see if they have re-found their own.

2. The children sit and watch while you place all their pictures face down on the floor. Hand out Picture Code Cards in random order. Each child takes a turn guessing where the matching picture is on the floor, and 'wins' it, if correct.

3. If a child chooses the wrong picture, and it can be blended with the one in hand, he/she should say them together.

4. Place all pictures face up. Ask: "Who can bring me all the letters for **dog**?" etc.

Xmas Stockings

Place objects (or pictures) of things each Letterland character would like (because it starts with their sound), e.g. kite for the king, jack-in-the-box for Jim, etc.

Sentence Building

Make up short sentences from words used so far, e.g.

I am glad.
Is Fred fat?
We can win.

Divide the children into groups (seven, eight or nine children to match the number of letters in the sentence).

Hand out one plain letter per child. First each child draws the Letterland character on to the letter. Then the group tries to work out words to create the sentence. Capital letters, full stops and question marks all give them clues.

Cut out their letters. Help them to mount and read each other's sentences.

Re-read First Dictionary Words

The dictionary entries should so far include a minimum of the following words, and hopefully, many more.

a – at, add	**i** – it, is, I	**q** – quick	**x/y/z** – (six, next)
b – bat, bed	**j** – jam, jet, jacket	**r** – red, run, ran	– yes, yet
c – cat, can	**k** – kick, kiss, king	**s** – sad, sat	– zip, zebra
d – dad	**l** – leg, lots, lost	**t** – tap, tick	
e – end, egg	**m** – mat, man	**u** – up	**a,e,i,o,u** – all words
f – fat, fit	**n** – not, net: no	**v** – velvet	on Code Sheets 27 – 31
g – gas, go	**o** – on	**w** – wet, will went	
h – hat, ham	**p** – pat, pet, pot	**wh** – when	**o** – come, some, etc.

Each child should be able to read all entries. Any child who cannot should receive help to ensure success before many new words are entered, both for reading and for spelling purposes.

Make a Popularity Graph

The children vote for their favourite character and set out the results on a graph. Many opportunities for discussion are generated by such a 'popularity poll', involving letters and number concepts.

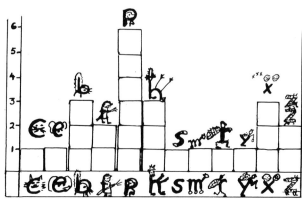

Graph made by children at Chatworth Infants School, Hounslow, using these 12 letters as candidates for their votes.

Ear First Game: Phase 3

Play as described on page 43. Use different lists on different days.

These combinations are more difficult. Again, watch out for the children who have difficulty. Their hearing may need checking, or they may need more exercises like these to improve their auditory discrimination.

First have the children make the following cards, plain on one side and coded on the other: **pP/bB**; **vV/wW**; **rR/lL**; **cC/gG** (already made); **iI/eE** and **oO/uU**.

p/b	v/w	r/l
potato	varnish	rhyme and rhythm
broken basket	warning	lullaby
pinpoint	violin	restaurant
bubbles	waste	light load
postman	visor	rough ride
big bonfire	wobble	loft
price	visitor	radiator
brakes	wet washing	life line
printed papers	vegetables	rising rocket
bits and bobs	warning	label

c/g	i/e	o/u
cold carrots	impossible	understand
glass greenhouse	envelope	on and on
careful climber	illness	upside down
garden gloves	elbow	oblong
clever clown	infant	uncle
cosy cot	endless	ostrich
garage	interesting	undone
crusty crumbs	edge	otter
grey gull	immediately	unfortunate
grateful granny	ever so	olives

Looking Ahead

You have now completed your introduction of the alphabet. In the perspective of English language teaching as a whole this is, of course, only the end of the beginning. This far the children have (hopefully) learned the following.

● How to read short-vowel words with ease.
● How to alternate between 'sight' and 'sounding out' reading strategies, according to need.
● That words have recurring letter patterns within them, worth looking out for at the start.
● That letters may change their sound in specific sequences.
● That these changes are interesting (rather than frustrating).
● That words carry messages, alone, in phrases and in sentences.
● That words, whether regular or irregular, can be fun to spell.

What comes next, in the Main Pack, has already been foreshadowed in this Starter Pack in the treatment of **ng, wh** and **sh** and of high usage words like **what, of** and **off**.

At this next stage, Pictograms really come into their own, as they take the children securely into the thousands of words where the original 26 letters combine to represent new sounds. These new sounds – in over 60 new spelling patterns – are simply the result of interaction between already well-known Letterland characters.

Learning how to *predict* the value of any vowel in an unknown word affords children a giant step towards literacy. These predicting strategies form an important feature of the Main Pack. They include important general principles of word structure such as the Magic E, Vowels Out Walking (**ai, ea, oa,** etc.), Witch Controlled Vowels (**aw, ow, ew,** etc.), Robber Controlled Vowels (**ar, er, ir, or, ur** and **oor, our** etc.) and others.

Each of them will bring thousands of words into the children's reading vocabulary and simultaneously inform and guide their progress in spelling.

The Main Pack can be linked to any number of other reading materials. Its aim is to ensure that, no matter what the children read or write, they will know enough about letter behaviour to interact with words comfortably. This is the pre-condition for real enjoyment of the English language.

Section 3

The following Appendix is for quick reference. In it, you will find details of the handwriting verses to be used with each Step – ready to be photocopied and taken home one by one by the children. You will also find song details for each letter, plus instructions for using the 'Listen and Write Sheets' and 'Code Sheets', and for those items you need to make. Finally, there is a brief coverage of how to code children's names – an important act for any child.

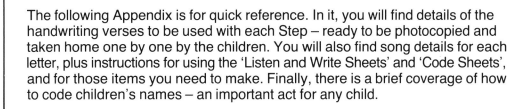

Worksheet Instructions

LISTEN AND WRITE SHEETS FOR A-Z

Photocopy either the top or bottom half of any master sheet so that it becomes the top half of a new A4 sheet. Have the children practise the sound under study and colour all pictures except the odd-one-out (the **u** and **qu** have no odd ones). Use the odd-one-out for discussion and comparison with the shape and sound of the featured letter. Use the lower half as you wish. Suggestions are given below.

Master Sheet 1 showing lower half ready for your exercises.

Two Master sheets. Separate by copying one half only.

Copy of top half with blank lower half showing space for exercises.

Copy of lower half moved to top.

Suggestions

● Add letters in coloured felt pens in different sizes beside each object. Let the children overwrite them. Use lower half for handwriting practice.

● Add words on lower half for children to match to the pictures, fill in the missing letter, and ring the odd one out.

● Add pairs of words for children to choose from next to the object, striking off the one that does not apply. Use lower half for sentences about the objects.

● Add six lines, date the sheet and send it home for parents and children to talk about together. Ask the parents to supervise handwriting practice on rough paper, then have the child add his or her very best efforts on this sheet *one row per week*. After six weeks, progress in pencil control and neatness should show up for everyone to commend.

● Photocopy any of the master sheets with letters and pictures just as they stand on both halves. Send them home and ask parents to:

  1. Talk about the pictures, helping the child to compare the two letter shapes and their sounds.
  2. Have the child ring the odd-ones-out and draw an arrow to the section where they really belong. The child colours the objects and returns the sheet next day to keep in a Letterland folder.

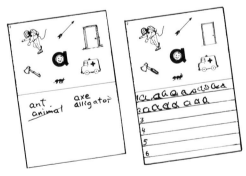

148

CODE SHEETS

On these code sheets some of your most important teaching will take place.
Normally, young readers' eyes linger only for seconds on any particular word, especially if they are, quite rightly, trying to read for meaning. It is only when they **re-read** that, strengthened by their success in receiving the message, they can feel free to pay real attention to the medium.

These sheets are carefully graded to allow you to make re-reading into a time for savouring sounds; a time for the children to discover and celebrate the existence of particular letters within now familiar, meaningful words, by animating them with their picture coding.

Accent on Language
First discuss the illustrations. Lists marked 'Oral' in each STEP give you handy words to stimulate discussion and provide vocabulary enrichment.

Accent on Meaning (First Readings)
You read the words on the Code Sheet under study. The children repeat them. You re-read and encourage them to point to the words, guided by the pictures.

Accent on Listening (Second Readings)
Focus on the sound under study. First the children listen for it in *your* voice. (Slightly exaggerate the sound as you read.)

Next they listen for it in *their own* voices as they repeat the words.

Accent on Coding (Further Readings)
Each child confirms hearing the sound by overwriting and then animating the letter. Each act of picture coding becomes:
● A form of highlighting.
● A confirmation of a particular sound perceived, noted and attended to right within the word where it occurs.

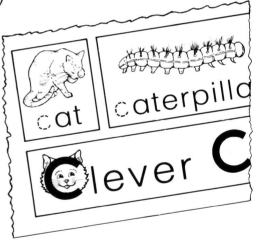

Once a letter is coded, the children have, by their own hands, virtually enabled themselves to 'see' that letter's sound.

Accent on Consolidation
On re-reading each earlier sheet, the child is looking for the latest sound learnt, carefully observing it in its special position in various words. The right sheets to re-read are listed in the Code Sheet sections of each STEP, together with other useful teaching points.

(Continued over.)

550 Word Start

By re-reading and entering into the Code Sheet vocabulary with their drawings, your beginner readers will soon have a core vocabulary of 320 words to their credit. Flashcards, action sentences and word building activities will quickly bring this figure to 550 plus.

The children will also be approaching words in *any book that they then read* with a resourcefulness which teachers working within any 'plain letter' teaching programme simply cannot hope to expect.

PICTURE CODING

Explain to the children at the start that the reason for listening to a sound in a word *before* picture coding a letter, is to make sure that the picture they are going to add *matches* the letter's sound. They will find a few exceptions. (These exceptions are included to ensure that they do not just picture code a letter without thinking about its sound). *Stress the importance of taking good care of each sheet, as each one will be needed again and again.*

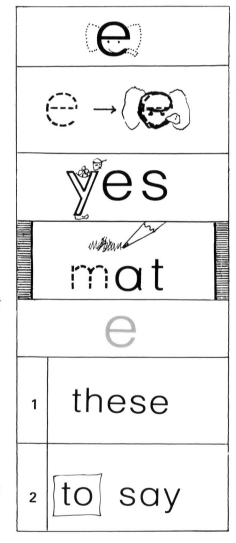

Solid Letters. Dots indicate where the children should overwrite the drawings (add the picture code).

Broken Line Letters. The children overwrite these first in a *dark* colour. They then code them in a contrasting bright colour. Where only a few colours are available, thick black, thin red, orange and light blue will be enough. If possible use the colours specified for each code sheet in each Step.

Hollow Letters. Fill with that letter's colour, or the nearest available colour.

Empty Spaces. The children study the word under an empty box, then draw in its meaning.

Grey Letters. (Mainly **e**'s). Grey denotes silent symbols. Do *not* picture code them. No picture applies because they have no sound.

Sight Words. A few words cannot be coded yet, because they contain more advanced sounds. You have two choices.
  1 Simply leave their irregular parts uncoded.
  2 Have the children draw a box around the whole word.

By boxing the whole word a child reinforces the idea that their eyes should take this particular word in as a whole. Sight words used are: **the, this, that, to** and a few words ending in **-er, -y** and silent **e**.

The character names are mostly regular but a few also have irregular parts. The chief function of the character names is to teach capital letter recognition and sight reading as a strategy. So simply ignore new sounds such as the **ou** and soft **c** in Bouncy.

Draw attention to the following:

Word Shape. Not only the initial letter but also overall shape and length help to identify a word.

Letter Position. The letter under study can be in several places at once. It can even appear twice in the same word.

Capital Letters. Discuss and compare capital and small letter shapes when appropriate.

Compare Words. Select one or two words to set out on your Picture Code Cards before you begin each new Code Sheet. Also select enough cards for the children to construct more afterwards, by swapping the cards around.

Accept with equal enthusiasm any non-words they may happen to make. Help them to pronounce them and laugh at their funny sounds together.

The children may like to colour in the illustrations when they have finished picture coding the letter under study.

Code Sheet 21

HOW TO USE THE CONSONANT CAPERS

Use each 'Caper' IN ANY ORDER to suit your children's needs.
The tunes are in Songbook and Tape 2A. *See Page 159.*

The Handwriting Verses

These verses help children to 'map on to' the **core** shape of each letter – the shapes vital for reading print in books. First make sure they have learned these **core** strokes. Then it will be safe to introduce cursive join lines without risk of confusion. At that later point help them to convert pictogram details such as shoes (**l**, **t**) and hair (**q**) into join lines.

Suggestions

● The children chant or sing the verses while air tracing the strokes (see Letterland Songbook and Audio Tape One). Encourage them to imagine the Letterland characters within the letters as they trace.

● Send the verses home, one by one, so that the parents can help with handwriting practice and repeat the verse together with the child until it is virtually memorised.

● Later re-use the verses as little sight reading exercises. Like nursery rhymes, they will become easy reading because the words are already so familiar.

At the leaf begin.
Go round the apple this way.

Then add a line down,
so Annie won't roll away

Brush down Ben's
big, long ears.

Go up and round his head
so his face appears!

Curve round Clever Cat's
face to begin,

Then gently tickle her
under her chin.

Draw Dippy Duck's back.
Go round her tum.

Go up to her head.
Then down you come!

Ed has a headband.
Draw it and then,

stroke round his head
and his trunk to the end.

First draw Fred's helmet.
Then go down his clothes.

Give him some arms
so he can hold his hose.

Go round Golden Girl's head.
Go down her golden hair.

Then curve to make her swing
so she can sit there.

Hurry from the Hat Man's head
down to his heel on the ground.

Go up and bend his knee over,
so he'll hop while he makes his sound.

Inside the ink bottle
draw a line.

Add an inky dot.
That's fine!

Just draw down Jim,
bending his knees.

Then add the one ball
which everyone sees.

Kicking King's body
is a straight stick.

Add his arm, then his leg,
so he can KICK!

Lamp Lady looks
like one straight line.

Go straight from head to foot
and she's ready to shine!

Make Munching Mike's back leg first,
then his second leg, and third,

so he can go munch-munching
in a word.

"Now bang my nail,"
Naughty Nick said.

"Go up and over
a-round my head."

On Oscar Orange
start at the top.

Go all the way round him,
and .... then stop.

Pat Poor Peter properly.
First stroke down his ear,

then up and round his face
so he won't shed a tear.

Quickly go round
the Queen's cross face.

Then comb her beautiful
hair into place.

Run down Robber Red's body.
Go up, to his arm and his hand.

Then watch out for this robber
roaming round Letterland.

Start at Sam's head
where he can see.

Stroke down to his tail,
oh so care-ful-ly!

Tall as a tower
make Ticking Tom stand.

Go from head to toe,
and then from hand to hand.

Under the umbrella
draw a shape like a cup.

Then draw a straight line
so it won't tip up.

Very neatly,
start at the top.

Draw down your vase,
then up, and stop.

When you draw the Witch's wells,
where she works her wicked spells,

whizz down and up and then ...,
whizz down and up again.

Fix two sticks,
to look like this.

That's how to draw
a little kiss.

You first make the yo-yo sack
on the Yo-yo Man's back,

and then go down to his toes
so he can sell his yo-yos.

Zip across Zig Zag's nose.
Stroke her neck...,

stroke her back....
Zzzoom! Away she goes.

Singsong for Letter Sounds

Words by Lyn Wendon and Vivien Stone

Familiar nursery tunes are a popular and effective vehicle for Letterland verses which practise each letter's sound. A leader holds up each Picture Code Card, first plain side, then Pictogram side, and announces the character. The leader may be the teacher, or 26 children, each taking a turn at announcing one letter. All children then sing about each letter. Produced in an assembly, children of all ages usually enjoy joining in. (It takes approximately 20 minutes to sing them all.)*

Tune: Here We Go Round the Mulberry Bush
This is the way to Letterland, Letterland, Letterland.
This is the way to Letterland, so come and follow me.
We shall meet with all our friends, all our friends, all our friends.
We shall meet with all our friends, just you wait and see!

Annie Apple say ă . . . in words,
ă . . . in word, ă in words,
Annie Apple says ă . . . in words.
She belongs to Mr A.

Bouncy Ben says b . . . in words,
b . . . in words, b . . . words,
Bouncy Ben say b . . . in words,
before he hides in his burrow.

Clever Cat say c . . . * in words,
c . . . * in words, c . . . * in words,
Clever Cat say c . . . * in words,
and cuddles close to me.

She also make another sound,
another sound, another sound.
She also makes another sound.
Just you wait and see.

Tune: London Bridge

D . . d . . d . . goes Dippy Duck,
Dippy Duck, Dippy Duck.
D . . d . . d . . goes Dippy Duck,
All duck down.

Eddy El-e-phant say ĕ . . .,
ĕ . . ., ĕ . . ., ĕ . . .; ĕ . . ., ĕ . . ., ĕ .
Eddy Elephant says ĕ . . .,
He belongs to Mr E.

Ffff, fff, fff goes Fireman Fred,
Fireman Fred, Fireman Fred.
Ffff, fff, fff goes Fireman Fred,
fighting fires with foam.

Tune: Have you seen the Muffin Man

Golden Girl say g . . . in words,
g . . . in words, g . . . in words.
Golden Girl says g . . . in words,
gigg-ling merrily.

Her girlfriend makes another sound,
another sound, another sound.
Her girlfriend makes another sound,
Just you wait and see.

The Hat Man whispers hhh* in words,
hhh* in words, hhh* in words.
The Hat Man whispers hhh* in words.
He will not talk out loud.

Impy Ink says ĭ . . . in words,
ĭ . . . in word, ĭ . . . in words.
Impy Ink says ĭ . . . in words.
He belongs to Mr I.

Tune: Old MacDonald Had a Farm

Jumping Jim says j . . . in words,
as he jumps along. (Repeat)
With a j . . j . . here, and a j . . j . . there;
here; a j . . there a j . .,
everywhere a j . . j . .
Jumping Jim says j . . in words
as he jumps along.

Kicking King say k . . .* in words,
as he kicks along. (Repeat)
With a k . . k . .* here, and a k . . k . .*
there; here a k . .*, there a k . .*,
everywhere a k . . k . .*. Kicking King
says k . .* in words, as he kicks along.

Tune: Twinkle, Twinkle, Little Star
Look, look, look, that lovely light.
It's Lamp Lady's light so bright.
Listen; "Lll . . ." is what she'll say.
"Lll . . ." for lamp, both night and day.
Look, look, look, that lovely light.
It's Lamp Lady's light so bright.

Mmmm, that monster 'Munching Mike',
My, he has an appetite.
Mmmm, he hums contentedly,
munching mouthfuls merrily.
Mmmm, that monster 'Munching Mike'.
My, he has an appetite!

Naughty Nick is a naughty lad.
Sometimes he's nice, but then he's bad.
Notice Naughty Nick says 'nnn'.
Notice Naughty Nick says 'nnn'.
Naughty Nick is a naughty lad.
Sometimes he's nice, but then he's bad.

End of Singsong Audio Tape: Side A

Singsong Audio Tape: Side B

Tune: The Muffin Man

Oscar Orange says ŏ in words;
ŏ in words, ŏ in words.
Oscar Orange say ŏ in words.
He belongs to Mr O.

Poor, poor Peter just says p . . .*,
just says p . . .*, just says p . . .*,
Poor, poor Peter just says p . . .*,
his poor, poor ears just droop. *
(Emphasise last p: but avoid 'puh'.)

Quarrelsome Queen says qu . . in words,
qu . . . in words, qu . . . in words.
Quarrelsome Queen says qu . . . in words.
She must have her umbrella.

Tune: Three Blind Mice

Rob-ber Red, Rob-ber Red. See how he runs.
See how he runs. He rrreally makes a
growling sound. He rrreally makes a
growling sound. Rrr, rrr, rrr. Rrr, rrr, rrr.

Tune: Old MacDonald Had a Farm
Sammy Snake says ssss . . .* in words,
hissing all the time. (Repeat)
With a sss-sss* here and a sss-sss* there,
here a sss*, there a sss*, everywhere a
sss-sss*; Sammy Snake says sss* in words.
Sss, sss, sss, ssss, sssss*.

Ticking { Tess / or / Tom } says t . . .* in words,
ticking all the time. (Repeat)
With a t . . t . .* here and a t . . t . .* there,
here a t . .*, there a t . .*, everywhere a t . ., t.
Ticking Tess (or Tom) says t . . .* in words,
T . . ., t . . ., t . . ., t . . ., t . .*.

Tune: Mary Had a Little Lamb
Uppy Umbrella says ŭ in words,
ŭ in words, ŭ in words.
Uppy Umbrella says ŭ in words.
She belongs to Mr. U.

This little vase says vvv . . . in words,
vvv . . . in words, vvv . . . in words.
This little vase says vvv . . . in words.
We hope it won't fall over.

Tune: Roll, Roll, Roll Your Boat

Www . . www . . www . . Wwwhat's that?
The Wicked Witch. Watch out for
her windy sound, the Wicked Witch!

Tune: The Muffin Man

Now let's whisper, whisper 'k-ss*',
whisper 'k-ss*', whisper 'k-ss*'.
Now let's whisper, whisper 'k-ss*',
for this nice, loving let-ter.
(No music: 'k-ss'.)

Tune: Baa, baa, black sheep
Yo-yo Man says y . . . in words.
Yyyes sir, yes sir, y . . . in words.
Yellow Yo-yos he will sell, and work for
other men as well. (Repeat first lines.)

Zig Zag Zebra is very shy.
She says 'zzz' while zzzipping by.
Zebras always will be shy, tho' we
never will know why. (Repeat first lines).

Final Tune: Mulberry Bush
Now we have been to Letterland,
Letterland, Letterland.
Now we have been to Letterland,
a special place to be.

But there are lots more sounds to learn,
sounds to learn, sounds to learn:
But there are lots more sounds to learn.
Just you wait and see!

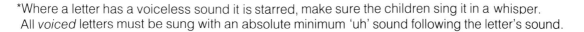

*Where a letter has a voiceless sound it is starred, make sure the children sing it in a whisper.
All *voiced* letters must be sung with an absolute minimum 'uh' sound following the letter's sound.

Actions to Accompany the A – Z

Once the songs are familiar, combine them with these actions to serve three purposes.
1. To consolidate the letters' sounds while practising the actions.
2. To strengthen associations through body movement.
3. To provide interest for any audience invited to listen to the songs.

In assembly some children may sing while others provide the actions, either one child at a time, or all miming the same letter. Add costumes, masks and other props for greater effect.

Important   When children impersonate the letters in front of others, make sure that they think of the wall behind them as a big imaginary page. Then their orientation for the Reading Direction will be the same as that of their audience. If, instead, they think of their 'page' as out in the audience, they will reverse their letter or letter order from the audience's point of view.

a	Bob up and down like an apple on a branch.	**n**	Bang imaginary nails, or make **n** shape over nose with left hand.
Mr A	Pick apples and put them in an imaginary apron.	**o**	Cup hands in **o**-shape, or turn somersaults.
b	Bounce, arms stretched straight.	**Mr O**	Hobble like an old man and wave right hand.
c	Stroke imaginary whiskers, or go on all fours.	**p**	Walk sadly drooping head and arms (ears).
d	Flap elbows and waddle.	**qu**	Stomp against Reading Direction followed by an umbrella child.
e	Two children make front and back of elephant. Front child swings arms for trunk.	**r**	Run, or prowl stealthily, sack over shoulder.
		s	Slither on floor, rising into **s**-shape.
Mr E	Take off imaginary hat and bow.	**t**	Turn on tiptoe, arms out-stretched.
f	Hold imaginary hose, arms close to chest.	**u**	Carry imaginary or real umbrella.
g	Sit or sit working feet for Go-Car.	**Mr U**	March proudly as though in uniform.
h	Hop along arms at sides.	**v**	Make **v**-shape with elbows together, hands apart.
i	Dip imaginary pen and write.	**w**	Pretend to be a witch, looking wicked.
Mr I	Lick imaginary ice-cream, wave.	**x**	One child, or two, blow kisses, and cross arms.
j	Jump with both knees bending and elbows out.	**y**	Work an imaginary yo-yo.
k	Kick leg and raise arm repeatedly.	**z**	Canter, anti-clockwise. Look shy.
l	Walk stiffly in tiny steps, smiling brightly.	**-ve**	**v**-child totters while **e**-child props him or her up, covering own mouth with other hand.
m	Three children make a monster. Head munches as they move.		